11+ Verbal Reasoning

For GL Assessment

This CGP book is brilliant for children aged 9-10 who are working towards the GL 11+. It's set at a slightly easier level than the real test — perfect for building confidence.

The first few sections are packed with topic-based questions that'll help them get to grips with each crucial skill. Once they've mastered those, they can move on to the mixed-topic Assessment Tests for more realistic 11+ practice.

There are also detailed answers at the back of the book to make marking as simple as possible!

How to access your free Online Edition

This book includes a free Online Edition to read on your PC, Mac or tablet. You'll just need to go to **cgpbooks.co.uk/extras** and enter this code:

2898 3252 9804 8087

By the way, this code only works for one person. If somebody else has used this book before you, they might have already claimed the Online Edition.

Practice Book – Ages 9-10

with Assessment Tests

How to use this Practice Book

This book is divided into two parts — themed question practice and assessment tests. There are answers and detailed explanations at the back of the book.

Themed question practice

- Each page contains practice questions divided by theme. Use these pages to work out your child's strengths and the areas they find tricky. The questions get harder down each page.

- Some questions are labelled 'Key Questions'. These come up in the most common tests.

- Your child can use the smiley face tick boxes to evaluate how confident they feel with each topic.

Assessment tests

- The second half of the book contains seven assessment tests, each with a mix of key question types from the first half of the book. They take a similar form to the real test.

- You can print multiple-choice answer sheets so your child can practise the tests as if they're sitting the real thing — visit cgpbooks.co.uk/11plus/answer-sheets or scan the QR code.

- Use the printable answer sheets if you want your child to do each test more than once.

- If you want to give your child timed practice, give them a time limit of 40 minutes for each test, and ask them to work as quickly and carefully as they can.

- The tests get harder from 1-7, so don't be surprised if your child finds the later ones more tricky.

- Your child should aim for a mark of around 85% (51 questions correct) in each test. If they score less than this, use their results to work out the areas they need more practice on.

- If they haven't managed to finish the test in time, they need to work on increasing their speed, whereas if they have made a lot of mistakes, they need to work more carefully.

- Keep track of your child's scores using the progress chart at the back of the book.

Published by CGP

Editors:
Claire Boulter, Heather Gregson, Holly Poynton, Jo Sharrock

Contributors:
Jane Bayliss

With thanks to Luke von Kotze and Samantha Bensted for the proofreading.

Please note that CGP is not associated with GL Assessment in any way. This book does not include any official questions and is not endorsed by GL Assessment.

ISBN: 978 1 78908 166 4

Printed by Elanders Ltd, Newcastle upon Tyne
Clipart from Corel®

Based on the classic CGP style created by Richard Parsons.

Text, design, layout and original illustrations © Coordination Group Publications Ltd. (CGP) 2018
All rights reserved.

Photocopying this book is not permitted, even if you have a CLA licence.
Extra copies are available from CGP with next day delivery • 0800 1712 712 • www.cgpbooks.co.uk

Contents

Tick off the check box for each topic as you go along.

Section One — The Alphabet

Alphabet Positions .... 2 ☑
Identify a Letter from a Clue .... 3 ☐
Alphabetical Order .... 4 ☐

Section Two — Making Words

Missing Letters .... 5 ☐
Move a Letter .... 6 ☐
Hidden Word .... 7 ☐
Find the Missing Word .... 8 ☐
Use a Rule to Make a Word .... 9 ☐
Compound Words .... 10 ☐
Forming New Words .... 11 ☐
Complete a Word Pair .... 12 ☐
Anagram in a Sentence .... 13 ☐
Words that Can't be Made .... 14 ☐
Word Ladders .... 15 ☐

Section Three — Word Meanings

Closest Meaning .... 16 ☐
Opposite Meaning .... 17 ☐
Multiple Meanings .... 18 ☐
Odd Ones Out .... 19 ☐
Word Connections .... 20 ☐
Reorder Words to
Make a Sentence .... 21 ☐

Section Four — Maths and Sequences

Complete the Sum .... 22 ☐
Letter Sequences .... 23 ☐
Number Sequences .... 24 ☐
Related Numbers .... 25 ☐
Letter-Coded Sums .... 26 ☐

Section Five — Logic and Coding

Letter-Word Codes .... 27 ☐
Number-Word Codes .... 28 ☐
Explore the Facts .... 30 ☐
Solve the Riddle .... 32 ☐
Letter Connections .... 34 ☐
Word Grids .... 35 ☐

Assessment Tests

Test 1 .... 36 ☐
Test 2 .... 41 ☐
Test 3 .... 46 ☐
Test 4 .... 51 ☐
Test 5 .... 56 ☐
Test 6 .... 61 ☐
Test 7 .... 66 ☐

Answers .... 71 ☐
Progress Chart .... 86 ☐

Section One — The Alphabet

Alphabet Positions

Answer the questions below. Use the alphabet to help you.

A B C D E F G H I J K L M N O P Q R S T U V W X Y Z

Look at this example:

> Which letter is at position **2** in the alphabet?   **B**

Hint: Using a pencil to cross out letters in the alphabet might help you to answer these questions.

1. Which letter is at position **3** in the alphabet?   _____

2. Which letter is at position **24** in the alphabet?   _____

3. If the alphabet was written backwards, which letter would be at position **1**?   _____

4. If the alphabet was written backwards, which letter would be at position **12**?   _____   / 4

What is the alphabet position of the first letter of the word:

5. **GUNGE?**   _____

6. **HOUSE?**   _____

What is the alphabet position of the last letter of the word:

7. **SLIMY?**   _____

8. **NITWIT?**   _____   / 4

9. If all the letters in the word **CHEESE** were removed from the alphabet, which letter would be in position **3** of the new alphabet?   _____

10. If all the letters in the word **RABBIT** were removed from the alphabet, what alphabet position would the letter **Y** occupy?   _____

11. If all the letters from the word **SHARK** were removed from the alphabet, which letter would be in position **10** of the new alphabet?   _____

12. If all the letters in the word **FOGHORN** were removed from the alphabet, what alphabet position would the letter **J** occupy?   _____   / 4

Identify a Letter from a Clue

Find the letter that the clue refers to.
Make sure your answer is correct for all parts of the clue.

Look at this example:

Find the letter that occurs most often in **CANNONBALL**.   __N__

Find the letter that occurs:

1. three times in **HUBBUB**. ____

2. most often in **AVALANCHE**. ____

3. most often in **PREDECESSOR**. ____

4. twice in **ABANDON** and three times in **AARDVARK**. ____

5. most often in **INDIVIDUAL**. ____

/ 5

6. twice in **ACCIDENT** and twice in **SPECIFIC**. ____

7. once in **SLOBBER** and twice in **RARITY**. ____

8. once in **POODLE** and twice in **LENTIL**. ____

9. twice in **LECTURER** and twice in **LESSER**. ____

10. twice in **ARRANGE** and twice in **TOMORROW**. ____

/ 5

11. twice in **TERRAPIN**, twice in **RARIFY** and twice in **HORRIBLE**. ____

12. three times in **INNOCENT**, twice in **NOMINATE** and twice in **SNOWMAN**. ____

Hint: Make sure you look at all the words in the question before you write your answer.

13. twice in **KERFUFFLE**, three times in **VENERABLE** and twice in **ELECTRIC**. ____

14. twice in **RUMPUS**, twice in **TRUCULENT** and twice in **UNANIMOUS**. ____

/ 4

Section One — The Alphabet

Alphabetical Order

Answer the questions below. Use the alphabet to help you.

A B C D E F G H I J K L M N O P Q R S T U V W X Y Z

Look at this example:

> Which letter in the word **PUPPY** comes nearest the end of the alphabet? ___Y___

If you arrange the following words in alphabetical order, which comes third?

1. Sneak, Strap, Slips, Sandy, Soapy   _____
2. Bulls, Beard, Brown, Birth, Bless   _____

If you arrange the following words in alphabetical order, which comes fourth?

3. Drops, Drape, Dream, Drown, Drain   _____
4. Flower, Flames, Flapper, Flipper, Floats _____

/ 4

5. Which letter in the word **PORTLY** comes nearest the end of the alphabet? _____
6. Which letter in the word **JIGGLE** comes nearest the start of the alphabet? _____
7. Which letter in the word **INFANT** comes nearest the end of the alphabet? _____
8. Which letter in the word **WISELY** comes nearest the start of the alphabet? _____

/ 4

If you spell the following words backwards, then put them in alphabetical order, which word comes second?

Hint: Try spelling these words out backwards on a separate sheet of paper.

9. Tremor, Calendar, Player, Dreamer, Humour   _____
10. Biology, Calmly, Happily, Chemistry, Stretchy _____

If you spell the following words backwards, then put them in alphabetical order, which word comes third?

11. Playing, Drawing, Snoozing, Grinning, Glowing _____
12. Cabbage, Carriage, Damage, Spillage, Dressage _____

/ 4

Section One — The Alphabet

Section Two — Making Words

Missing Letters

Key Question: Find the letter that will finish the first word and start the second word of each pair. The same letter must be used for both pairs.

Look at this example:

kis (?) at   ga (?) et   _s_   (**kiss**, **sat**, **gas** and **set**.)

1. jaz (?) oo   fiz (?) ip   _____
2. hop (?) arl   fac (?) at   _____
3. tw (?) ff   to (?) ne   _____
4. ban (?) ite   hoo (?) ing   _____
5. fin (?) rop   pa (?) ot   _____
6. as (?) id   boo (?) ey   _____

Hint: Check that your letter fits with all four of the words before you write it down.

/ 6

7. tal (?) it   sil (?) ove   _____
8. pi (?) lue   clo (?) ood   _____
9. to (?) ver   pi (?) ar   _____
10. ma (?) ant   la (?) ut   _____
11. bus (?) ope   sas (?) ot   _____
12. mea (?) ose   pil (?) aw   _____

/ 6

13. sa (?) ay   ja (?) on   _____
14. bu (?) ow   pi (?) ice   _____
15. eas (?) ard   pa (?) awn   _____
16. si (?) ag   car (?) ale   _____
17. pa (?) in   se (?) et   _____
18. se (?) arn   mil (?) we   _____

/ 6

Move a Letter

Key Question: Remove one letter from the first word and add it to the second word to make two new words. Do not change the order of the other letters. Write the letter that moves on the line.

Look at this example:

fork   it   _k_ (The new words are **for** and **kit**.)

1. wart   arm   _____
2. find   in   _____
3. zoom   ate   _____
4. blame   ore   _____
5. done   well   _____
6. face   scar   _____

/ 6

7. fable   ail   _____
8. hard   are   _____
9. open   pint   _____
10. raft   act   _____
11. tease   sop   _____
12. bring   tale   _____

/ 6

13. port   ate   _____
14. spoil   ark   _____
15. cast   ilk   _____
16. amble   tie   _____
17. crave   oar   _____
18. tarn   pop   _____

Hint: If you can't see the answer at first, go through the letters in the first word one by one to see which one can be removed.

/ 6

Section Two — Making Words

Hidden Word

Key Question: In each sentence below a four-letter word is hidden at the end of one word and the start of the next. Underline the part of the sentence that contains the hidden word and write the hidden word on the line.

Look at this example:

Dad banged his <u>hip</u>.   <u>ship</u>

1. I lost my best hat. _____
2. I spent time at home. _____
3. No seats were left. _____
4. Sea monsters like eating cabbage. _____
5. The passengers swam ashore. _____
6. Fatima saw Ted after school. _____

/ 6

7. James will carry our bags. _____
8. Aarav took the fabric home. _____
9. The gremlin evaporated at once. _____
10. It's safe around the factory. _____
11. We saw koalas this morning. _____
12. Caleb asked for help. _____

/ 6

13. The zoo makes no profit. _____
14. Heather enjoys playing tennis. _____
15. Nana kept hugging me. _____
16. Jakub turned his phone on. _____
17. His shoelace was untied. _____
18. My teacher was eaten by a bear. _____

Hint: If you can't see the hidden word try writing out the sentence with no spaces — it might help you to spot it.

/ 6

Find the Missing Word

Key Question

Find the three-letter word that completes the word in capital letters, and so finishes the sentence in a sensible way. Write your answer on the line.

Look at this example:

> The **FER** milked his cows. ARM

Hint: Read the whole sentence before thinking about the missing word — it'll give you a clue to what the missing word might be.

1. The courier was **BIT** by the poodle. _____
2. When it snowed we had a **SBALL** fight. _____
3. I play the **TPET** in the school band. _____
4. Today is Saturday, so **TOMOR** is Sunday. _____
5. The hot air **BOON** sailed above the clouds. _____
6. Keep milk in the **FGE** so it stays cool. _____

/ 6

7. The diamond **GLITTE** in the sunlight. _____
8. The farmer drove her **TROR** through the fields. _____
9. I **PLED** some magic beans in the garden. _____
10. We live on **PLA** Earth. _____
11. Daffodils are a bright **YEL** colour. _____
12. My **GDMA** is 364 years old this year. _____

/ 6

13. The milkman **WTLED** a tune as he delivered his milk. _____
14. The sun cast a **SOW** on the sundial. _____
15. Mum grows potatoes and **CARS** in her vegetable patch. _____
16. I **BED** some water to make a cup of tea. _____
17. My T-shirt was the **MUDST** after we went bog-snorkelling. _____
18. The clock **CED** seven o'clock. _____

/ 6

Section Two — Making Words

Use a Rule to Make a Word

Key Question: The words in the second set follow the same pattern as the words in the first set. Find the missing word to complete the set.

Look at this example:

sum (sun) pin   sip (__sit__) cat

1. big (bin) tin   sad (_____) dig
2. fan (ant) tap   gel (_____) koi
3. mark (tar) tell   fort (_____) name
4. pile (top) atom   note (_____) scar
5. fall (lit) sift   time (_____) carp
6. bust (tub) trim   dump (_____) base

Hint: Check your answer is a real word — look it up in the dictionary if you're not sure.

/ 6

7. part (eat) tune   dark (_____) deal
8. miss (sin) dune   redo (_____) tank
9. rain (kin) rank   main (_____) mist
10. mile (lit) bits   mask (_____) tide
11. mice (rice) tore   tame (_____) tall
12. flip (lip) pink   came (_____) open

/ 6

13. boil (lob) able   ring (_____) ages
14. gape (peg) grip   fame (_____) task
15. bait (pat) tape   gave (_____) told
16. fond (din) rind   page (_____) limb
17. sigh (his) shin   doll (_____) foil
18. mess (same) bale   port (_____) more

/ 6

Compound Words

Key Question

Underline a word from the first set, followed by a word from the second set, that go together to form a new word.

Look at this example:

(<u>tea</u> pour milk)   (<u>cup</u> in glass)   (The word is **teacup**.)

1. (cake bath sponge)   (room shower handle)
2. (hop run leap)   (toad frog cat)
3. (frighten leave scare)   (swan crow hat)
4. (lady crew girl)   (dog hamster bird)
5. (jump ride hop)   (fruit scotch pole)
6. (cry tear whine)   (drop leave sad)

/ 6

7. (rail hill street)   (motorway bridge way)
8. (green black thistle)   (barrow berry light)
9. (over up under)   (jump line down)
10. (pony walking horse)   (boot bridle shoe)
11. (wheel car tractor)   (engine tyre chair)
12. (at on out)   (window door home)

/ 6

13. (house door window)   (sound number bell)
14. (black white tin)   (bored bird whistle)
15. (fear earth big)   (war quake sum)
16. (fright child man)   (kind ten nice)
17. (pony farm cow)   (tale milk yard)
18. (hum hymn bad)   (bird bug dog)

Hint: Watch out for words that go together but don't actually make a new word.

/ 6

Forming New Words

Find a word which, when put at the start or end of each set of three words, makes three new words. Write your answer on the line.

Look at this example:

| light | flower | dial | ___sun___ |

Find a word that can go **in front** of each of these words to form three new compound words:

1. pot   cake   spoon   _____
2. fall   bow   coat   _____
3. noon   shave   taste   _____
4. flake   ball   man   _____
5. castle   storm   box   _____
6. shore   shell   weed   _____
7. port   craft   bag   _____
8. berry   bird   mail   _____

/ 8

Hint: Make sure your answer works for all three of the words.

Find a word that can go **after** each of these words to form three new compound words:

9. blue   rasp   straw   _____
10. birth   week   to   _____
11. play   bed   day   _____
12. farm   green   light   _____
13. basket   net   eye   _____
14. day   street   moon   _____
15. humming blue   song   _____
16. juke   match   tool   _____

/ 8

Complete a Word Pair

Key Question: Find the word that completes the third pair of words so that it follows the same pattern as the first two pairs.

Look at this example:

| flagon   flag | market   mark | grinds   <u>grin</u> |

1. forest rest   attune tune   assail _____
2. boring ring   remove move   repeat _____
3. dragon drag   flower flow   shower _____
4. peachy each   brainy rain   covert _____
5. trap   part   stop   pots   loot   _____
6. adhere her   depend pen   malady _____

Hint: Look at both of the word pairs you're given — the letter pattern may be easier to spot in one than the other.

/ 6

7. pickle lick   bridge grid   hoopla _____
8. daft   deft   ball   bell   land   _____
9. dinner rid   pitted dip   pigeon _____
10. master ram   umpire emu   tatter _____
11. better bet   formal far   badger _____
12. carpet tar   jumper rum   petrol _____

/ 6

13. pimple limp   lament name   sample _____
14. tick   sick   nail   mail   game   _____
15. picnic nip   rigour our   manger _____
16. pedalo lope   resume mere   chalet _____
17. plants tap   drills lid   grinds _____
18. peek   peel   find   fine   loss   _____

/ 6

Section Two — Making Words

Anagram in a Sentence

Rearrange the letters in capitals to spell a word that completes the sentence in a sensible way. Write the new word on the line.

Look at this example:

The lion escaped from the **CSRICU**. ____CIRCUS____

Hint: If you're stuck, try writing the jumbled letters in a circle — it will make it easier to spot the correct word.

1. The prince killed the dragon with his **WORDS**. _____
2. Rebecca found a **GAGTOM** in her apple. _____
3. I visited a monastery and saw some **SMKNO**. _____
4. Our pet dinosaur has **ROGWN** very big recently. _____
5. I had to **SBRUC** the floor clean. _____
6. I **MWRADE** my soup in the microwave. _____

/ 6

7. The duchess wore a beautiful **VVTELE** dress. _____
8. I like to **VRTALE** by car. _____
9. I made the **TSWEEF** mistakes in the maths test. _____
10. The man **DDDNOE** in agreement. _____
11. I **SPUADE** my computer game when the phone rang. _____
12. The weather is **HRTTOE** in summer than in winter. _____

/ 6

13. Eating Brussels **OTSRPUS** makes you glow in the dark. _____
14. The **FIREGAF** had a very long neck. _____
15. I share my **ORODBEM** with my little brother. _____
16. The snake **HCERRAM** played his pipe. _____
17. Her ring had a huge **NIDDAOM** that gleamed in the sun. _____
18. The villain had a **NGNICNU** plan to take over the world. _____

/ 6

Section Two — Making Words

Words That Can't be Made

Underline the word that cannot be made using the letters from the word in capitals. The letters can only be used as many times as they occur in the word in capitals.

Look at this example:

| **FAIRLY** | air | fir | fly | <u>rat</u> | ray |

1. **EASILY**   sea   sit   sly   yes   lay
2. **COMPUTE**   put   cut   pet   met   ate
3. **BUCKETS**   set   tub   bat   bet   cub
4. **ARMBAND**   lad   arm   ram   man   ban
5. **ROCKETS**   sock   cost   tick   rose   sect
6. **DOLPHIN**   hind   dole   hold   plod   lion

Hint: Scan through the possible answers for a letter that is only in one word — this can be a quick way of spotting the word you're looking for.

/ 6

7. **TOASTER**   rats   star   tear   east   role
8. **HOGWASH**   gash   show   swag   gags   wash
9. **TRICKIER**   rate   kite   tick   tire   rice
10. **BREATHES**   beat   hate   bath   barb   stab
11. **CHAMBERS**   harm   meat   scar   sham   came
12. **GANGSTER**   tear   ants   rare   stag   sane

/ 6

13. **NIGHTMARE**   hint   mats   tear   hare   ream
14. **CAPTURES**   crate   spear   space   cuter   cores
15. **CARBUNCLE**   bear   clan   earn   crab   each
16. **HEADPHONES**   heads   hones   sheds   shape   shone
17. **LAWNMOWERS**   woman   meals   worse   walls   lawns
18. **POLLINATES**   later   plate   leaps   stain   plans

/ 6

Section Two — Making Words

Word Ladders

Change one letter at a time to make the first word into the final word. The two answers must be real words.

Look at this example:

FOOD (_FOND_) (_FIND_) FINE

1. HIDE (_____) (_____) WINK
2. MALE (_____) (_____) LIME
3. FAIL (_____) (_____) YELL
4. LOOM (_____) (_____) SORT
5. SILT (_____) (_____) PALE
6. CLIP (_____) (_____) PLAY

Hint: Only three of the letters change in each question. Work out which letter doesn't change and write it next to the question.

/ 6

7. HEAD (_____) (_____) HOLE
8. JOLT (_____) (_____) BELL
9. TENT (_____) (_____) RANK
10. JOKE (_____) (_____) POST
11. COAT (_____) (_____) FAST
12. MULE (_____) (_____) WORE

/ 6

13. CLOG (_____) (_____) FROM
14. HARP (_____) (_____) LORD
15. SPIN (_____) (_____) STUB
16. STAR (_____) (_____) FLAB
17. DIVE (_____) (_____) MODE
18. SLUM (_____) (_____) FLAP

/ 6

Section Two — Making Words

Section Three — Word Meanings

Closest Meaning

Key Question: Underline two words, one from each set of brackets, that have the most similar meaning.

Look at this example:

(<u>chat</u> joke hum)   (<u>talk</u> think listen)

1. (quiet angry glare)   (cross excited scared)
2. (smile laugh kind)   (scream nice yell)
3. (buy good sell)   (aim hello purchase)
4. (sweet sad ugly)   (foul sour pretty)
5. (crack allow calm)   (cold permit tidy)
6. (sing shout whisper)   (talk laugh murmur)

/ 6

7. (sensible annoying funny)   (laugh kind amusing)
8. (bin litter dust)   (clean garbage polish)
9. (cheap lovely precious)   (valuable poor grind)
10. (awful honest forget)   (argue sorry truthful)
11. (sunshine snow rain)   (wind cloud drizzle)
12. (same different better)   (worse identical wish)

/ 6

Hint: The two words don't have to mean exactly the same thing — they just have to be the most similar of all the options.

13. (talk wish imagine)   (hope fear observe)
14. (shape graph draw)   (write explain chart)
15. (cunning irritable slim)   (nasty vicious sly)
16. (accepting wishful friendly)   (amiable dream future)
17. (tidy dirty clean)   (cluttered neat work)
18. (accuse blame forgive)   (release pardon apology)

/ 6

Opposite Meaning

Key Question: Underline two words, one from each set of brackets, that have the most opposite meaning.

Look at this example:

(evening <u>dark</u> morning) (off paint <u>light</u>)

1. (cellar upstairs landing)   (downstairs hall kitchen)
2. (clean neat floor)   (carpet filthy trim)
3. (pretty young slender)   (crooked mean old)
4. (beautiful happy bright)   (boring hideous harsh)
5. (large over full)   (slim time empty)
6. (with wide high)   (right narrow tapering)

Hint: If you're not sure what a word means, look it up in the dictionary.

/ 6

7. (blush cuddle love)   (ignore sad loathe)
8. (hill river deep)   (water shallow stream)
9. (matt shiny soft)   (sturdy lean dull)
10. (peel stretch chop)   (wash squash slice)
11. (wealthy famous lucky)   (lonely poor gloomy)
12. (shop sell deal)   (borrow pay buy)

/ 6

13. (part main minor)   (much major some)
14. (tacky cheap bargain)   (rich costly lucky)
15. (enemy rebel villain)   (friend mentor colleague)
16. (crowd busy people)   (silent quiet still)
17. (taut baggy small)   (undone slack free)
18. (limp bumpy rocky)   (flat alive slippery)

/ 6

Section Three — Word Meanings

Multiple Meanings

Key Question: Choose the word that has a similar meaning to the words in both sets of brackets. Underline your answer.

Look at this example:

(serious solemn) (burial tomb)   coffin gloomy <u>grave</u>

Hint: The answer might be pronounced differently for the two different meanings.

1. (sugary syrupy) (lovely kind)   candy nice sweet
2. (drama show) (romp frolic)   musical play actor
3. (snug cramped) (mean stingy)   unfair tight poor
4. (summit peak) (lid cap)   mountain top hat
5. (overturn spill) (bother worry)   roll upset ask
6. (chilly icy) (unfriendly aloof)   cold mean freezing   /6

7. (plain natural) (easy clear)   straight simple hard
8. (now current) (gift offering)   ask present past
9. (class set) (application questionnaire)   type school form
10. (nice tender) (type sort)   group keep kind
11. (game contest) (pairing partnership)   match sport union
12. (autograph initial) (poster notice)   banner write sign   /6

13. (instant moment) (runner-up next)   day race second
14. (important major) (guide code)   key idea primary
15. (group orchestra) (ring circle)   band music join
16. (rubbish garbage) (deny decline)   trash refuse bin
17. (argue fight) (paddle sail)   row swim bicker
18. (pig boar) (seed plant)   piglet grow sow   /6

Odd Ones Out

Key Question

Three of the words in each list are linked. Underline the two words that are **not** related to these three.

Look at this example:

<u>Tom</u>   Kate   Jenny   <u>Jeremy</u>   Lucy

1. numbers   five   eleven   figures   seven
2. hot   freezing   warm   chilly   cold
3. like   hate   dislike   love   admire
4. whisper   shout   mutter   yell   scream
5. house   bungalow   office   flat   library
6. woodland   desert   glacier   rainforest   orchard

Hint: Remember the odd ones out don't have to be related to each other — they just have to be unrelated to the other three.

/ 6

7. lavender   grass   daffodil   lily   oak
8. cooker   oven   fridge   tiles   microwave
9. swings   slide   football   cricket   seesaw
10. violin   harp   recorder   guitar   trumpet
11. scarf   shorts   coat   mittens   sandals
12. happy   laugh   glad   pleased   chuckle

/ 6

13. shoes   socks   gloves   slippers   earrings
14. roast   diced   boiled   baked   peeled
15. sketch   portrait   orchestra   song   drawing
16. wool   fibreglass   leather   cotton   plastic
17. sing   rehearse   recite   perform   practice
18. enter   exit   leave   come   go

/ 6

Section Three — Word Meanings

Word Connections

Key Question: Choose two words, one from each set of brackets, that complete the sentence in the most sensible way. Underline both words.

Look at this example:

Dog is to (run eat <u>bark</u>) as **duck** is to (bread water <u>quack</u>).

Hint: Being able to recognise nouns, verbs and adjectives will help you to answer these questions. The answer will usually be two words of the same type.

1. **Carpet** is to (hard stain floor) as **curtain** is to (window glass hide).
2. **Right** is to (left mix correct) as **wrong** is to (incorrect bad wise).
3. **Ball** is to (dance tennis darts) as **shuttlecock** is to (hockey badminton tiddlywinks).
4. **Water** is to (drink café mug) as **food** is to (market eat full).
5. **Shout** is to (loud sing angry) as **whisper** is to (bored quiet old).
6. **Yawn** is to (happy angry tired) as **cry** is to (sad bored hungry).

/ 6

7. **Hard** is to (difficult soft solid) as **easy** is to (fun straightforward awful).
8. **Page** is to (bride pin book) as **website** is to (internet market friend).
9. **Fur** is to (soft warm cat) as **wool** is to (sheep pig cold).
10. **Present** is to (birthday here forget) as **absent** is to (school Easter away).
11. **Eight** is to (dog fish spider) as **four** is to (pig chicken wish).
12. **City** is to (shop walk big) as **village** is to (small flat pretty).

/ 6

13. **Flower** is to (bee fragrance petal) as **tree** is to (leaf climb green).
14. **King** is to (crown castle prince) as **queen** is to (frog princess fairy).
15. **Winter** is to (cold snow Christmas) as **summer** is to (beach school sun).
16. **Read** is to (calendar future book) as **watch** is to (film clock wrist).
17. **Frog** is to (hop croak green) as **sparrow** is to (garden feather fly).
18. **First** is to (win cheer gold) as **third** is to (next bronze silver).

/ 6

Section Three — Word Meanings

Reorder Words to Make a Sentence

Find the two words that should be swapped in order for each sentence to make sense. Underline both words.

Look at this example:

> I enjoy playing <u>Tom</u> with <u>tennis</u>.

Hint: Read the sentence out loud to help you work out which words have been swapped.

1. Season is my favourite winter.
2. I school to rode on a rhino.
3. Book this read for your homework tonight.
4. Look both ways when you road the cross.
5. Maths and subjects are my favourite Science.
6. The wooden darted under the cat table.

/ 6

7. We went France in camping last summer.
8. Put on your shoes before your socks.
9. The blue flag is French, white and red.
10. The ogre red on a munched apple.
11. Africa come from mongooses.
12. The whistle blew his referee at full-time.

/ 6

13. We won't station it to the make on time.
14. The circus opens night tomorrow.
15. The barge sailed gracefully canal the down.
16. Gemma early up got to go toe-wrestling.
17. Bus I'm taking the tomorrow to school.
18. The postman bag his carried of letters.

/ 6

Section Four — Maths and Sequences

Complete the Sum

Key Question

Find the missing number to complete each sum.
Write your answer on the line.

Look at this example:

9 × 3 = (_27_)

1. 20 ÷ 5 = (____)
2. 22 ÷ 11 = (____)
3. 5 × 5 = (____)
4. 8 + 13 = (____)
5. 10 × 2 = 24 − (____)
6. 15 ÷ 3 = 4 + (____)

Hint: Make sure you know your times tables inside out — it'll really help with these questions.

/ 6

7. 7 × 3 = 16 + (____)
8. 26 ÷ 2 = 20 − (____)
9. 24 ÷ 3 = 4 × (____)
10. 18 ÷ 6 = 9 ÷ (____)
11. 7 × 3 − 4 = (____)
12. 10 ÷ 5 + 2 = (____)

/ 6

13. 6 × 3 − 3 = (____)
14. 8 × 4 = 5 × 5 + (____)
15. 24 ÷ 3 × 5 = 4 × (____)
16. 15 × 2 ÷ 5 = (____) − 6
17. 12 ÷ 4 = 20 ÷ 4 − (____)
18. 25 ÷ 5 + 4 = 17 − (____)

/ 6

Letter Sequences

Find the pair of letters that continues each sequence in the best way. Use the alphabet to help you.

A B C D E F G H I J K L M N O P Q R S T U V W X Y Z

Look at this example:

AB BC CD DE EF (_FG_)

1. CS   CS   DT   DT   EU   (____)
2. NF   OE   PD   QC   RB   (____)
3. CJ   FM   IP   LS   OV   (____)
4. GR   HT   IV   JX   KZ   (____)
5. PE   RG   TI   VK   XM   (____)
6. CV   YZ   UD   QH   ML   (____)

/ 6

7. BS   DP   FM   HJ   JG   (____)
8. CA   AE   YI   WM   UQ   (____)
9. LL   ON   RP   UR   XT   (____)
10. US SP   QM   OJ   MG   (____)
11. ZV WS   TT   QQ   NR   (____)
12. CC DE   FG   GI   IK   (____)

/ 6

13. FT GO   LN   MI   RH   (____)
14. KJ MH   PE   RC   UZ   (____)
15. VJ TM   SO   QR   PT   (____)
16. AZ BV   DR   GN   KJ   (____)
17. EG GD   JB   LY   OW   (____)
18. YF TF   PG   MI   KL   (____)

Hint: Keep track of the sequence by jotting down whether each letter goes forwards or backwards, and by how many places.

/ 6

Section Four — Maths and Sequences

Number Sequences

Key Question

Find the number that continues each sequence in the best way. Write your answer on the line.

Look at this example:

| 1 | 3 | 5 | 7 | 9 | (_11_) |

1. 5   10   15   20   25   (____)
2. 1   2   4   8   16   (____)
3. 60   50   40   30   20   (____)
4. 7   14   21   28   35   (____)
5. 1   4   5   9   14   (____)
6. 8   12   12   16   16   (____)

Hint: Use a pencil to write the difference between each number in the sequence — it might help you spot the pattern.

/ 6

7. 4   4   8   12   20   (____)
8. 12   13   15   18   22   (____)
9. 96   48   24   12   6   (____)
10. 2   4   8   14   22   (____)
11. 1   10   2   15   3   20   (____)
12. 9   8   8   9   11   (____)

/ 6

13. 12   4   9   8   6   12   (____)
14. 2   3   6   11   18   (____)
15. 41   32   24   17   11   (____)
16. 2   2   4   12   (____)
17. 2   7   4   10   6   13   (____)
18. 50   37   26   17   10   (____)

/ 6

Related Numbers

Find the number that completes the final set of numbers in the same way as the first two sets. Write your answer on the line.

Look at this example:

6 (8) 2   5 (9) 4   10 (_13_) 3

1. 2 (5) 3   4 (9) 5   5 (____) 3
2. 12 (9) 3   6 (5) 1   13 (____) 5
3. 6 (15) 21   4 (17) 21   7 (____) 12
4. 2 (7) 12   4 (9) 14   8 (____) 18
5. 2 (8) 6   6 (16) 10   10 (____) 14
6. 8 (4) 0   24 (20) 16   32 (____) 24

Hint: Ignore any patterns between the three sets of numbers — just concentrate on how the numbers in each set are connected.

/ 6

7. 2 (8) 4   5 (40) 8   4 (____) 3
8. 9 (9) 18   11 (9) 20   14 (____) 23
9. 3 (2) 6   4 (3) 12   3 (____) 9
10. 14 (20) 26   3 (7) 11   15 (____) 21
11. 2 (4) 2   4 (12) 3   2 (____) 6
12. 10 (5) 2   9 (3) 3   12 (____) 4

/ 6

13. 8 (11) 14   15 (21) 27   28 (____) 36
14. 6 (36) 6   4 (16) 4   3 (____) 3
15. 12 (4) 4   18 (7) 3   24 (____) 6
16. 2 (14) 5   4 (20) 6   2 (____) 3
17. 10 (4) 2   8 (2) 4   20 (____) 8
18. 8 (12) 2   6 (4) 4   12 (____) 4

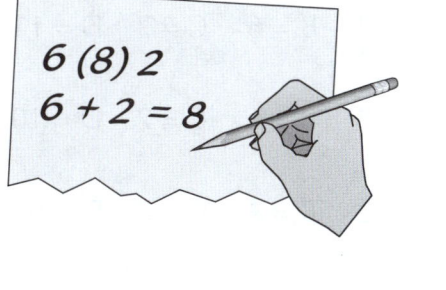

/ 6

Section Four — Maths and Sequences

Letter-Coded Sums

Each letter stands for a number. Work out the answer to each sum as a letter. Write your answer on the line.

Look at this example:

A = 1   B = 2   C = 3   D = 5   E = 8   E − D = (_C_)

1. A = 1   B = 3   C = 5   D = 7   E = 10   D + B = (____)

2. A = 2   B = 5   C = 6   D = 8   E = 12   E ÷ A = (____)

3. A = 1   B = 3   C = 7   D = 14   E = 17   E − D = (____)

4. A = 3   B = 5   C = 7   D = 15   E = 24   B × A = (____)

5. A = 2   B = 8   C = 16   D = 20   E = 25   C ÷ A = (____)

Hint: For these questions your answer must be a letter, not a number.

/ 5

6. A = 2   B = 7   C = 12   D = 14   E = 19   E − B + A = (____)

7. A = 3   B = 8   C = 9   D = 16   E = 20   A + B + C = (____)

8. A = 2   B = 3   C = 6   D = 12   E = 24   E ÷ B − C = (____)

9. A = 2   B = 5   C = 6   D = 13   E = 16   A × B + C = (____)

10. A = 2   B = 8   C = 12   D = 16   E = 24   D × A − B = (____)

/ 5

11. A = 4   B = 6   C = 7   D = 11   E = 13   A × B − E = (____)

12. A = 2   B = 6   C = 7   D = 10   E = 21   B × C ÷ E = (____)

13. A = 2   B = 4   C = 7   D = 9   E = 11   A × D − C − B = (____)

14. A = 1   B = 3   C = 4   D = 12   E = 13   B ÷ A × C + A = (____)

15. A = 2   B = 3   C = 9   D = 12   E = 16   A × B + D − E = (____)

/ 5

Section Five — Logic and Coding

Letter-Word Codes

Key Question

Each question uses a different code. Use the alphabet to help you work out the answer to each question.

A B C D E F G H I J K L M N O P Q R S T U V W X Y Z

Look at this example:

If the code for **TOE** is **SND**, what is the code for **FIB**? ___EHA___

Hint: Look out for mirror codes, where the letters are the same distance either side of the centre of the alphabet. A is a mirror of Z, B is a mirror of Y and so on — right through to M, which is a mirror of N.

1. If the code for **FISH** is **GJTI**, what is the code for **TANK**? _____

2. If the code for **ROSE** is **QNRD**, what is the code for **BUSH**? _____

3. If the code for **POST** is **NMQR**, what is **QJSE** the code for? _____

4. If the code for **STAR** is **VWDU**, what is the code for **MOON**? _____

5. If the code for **PINK** is **TMRO**, what is **FPYI** the code for? _____

/ 5

6. If the code for **METAL** is **LGSCK**, what is the code for **BRASS**? _____

7. If the code for **PHONE** is **SHRNH**, what is the code for **GHOUL**? _____

8. If code for **BROAD** is **DPQYF**, what is **UOWYV** the code for? _____

9. If the code for **ACE** is **ZXV**, what is **YZW** the code for? _____

10. If the code for **JELLY** is **LHNOA**, what is the code for **CREAM**? _____

/ 5

11. If the code for **ZANY** is **AZMB**, what is **XZIW** the code for? _____

12. If the code for **OTTER** is **OSRBN**, what is **MZPHO** the code for? _____

13. If the code for **CLASS** is **DJDOX**, what is the code for **TEACH**? _____

14. If the code for **BEND** is **YVMW**, what is **WIZD** the code for? _____

/ 4

Number-Word Codes

Key Question: The number codes for three of these four words are listed in a random order. Work out the code to answer the questions.

Hint: Words that start with the same letter will start with the same number in the codes.

BARN   ARID   BIND   BAND

1536   5324   1564

1. Find the code for the word **BIND**. _____1264_____

2. Find the code for the word **DRAB**. _____4351_____

3. Find the word that has the number code **1356**. _____BRAN_____

/ 3

TEAR   FOOT   FORE   FEAT

5112   5342   2346

4. Find the code for the word **TEAR**. _____2346_____

5. Find the code for the word **TORE**. _____2163_____

6. Find the word that has the number code **6452**. _____RAFT_____

/ 3

SEEK   SOAK   MAKE   ASKS

3554   1645   3264

7. Find the code for the word **SOAK**. _____3264_____

8. Find the code for the word **SAME**. _____3615_____

9. Find the word that has the number code **1634**. _____MASK_____

/ 3

ARCH   HAIR   RACE   HARE

6231   5261   5246

10. Find the code for the word **RACE**. _____6231_____

11. Find the code for the word **ACHE**. _____2351_____

12. Find the word that has the number code **3261**. _____CARE_____

/ 3

Number-Word Codes

Key Question: The number codes for three of these four words are listed in a random order. Work out the code to answer the questions.

LACK   WEAK   LEEK   LAKE

2564   1634   1554

13. Find the code for the word **LAKE**.   1645
14. Find the code for the word **CAKE**.   3645
15. Find the word that has the number code **4551**.   KEEL

/ 3

BEEN   ANEW   NAME   BANE

1665   5326   3564

16. Find the code for the word **ANEW**.   3564
17. Find the code for the word **MEAN**.   2635
18. Find the word that has the number code **4356**.   WANE

/ 3

MOAN   MEAN   MENU   OMEN

3654   6314   6542

19. Find the code for the word **OMEN**.   3654
20. Find the code for the word **NAME**.   4165
21. Find the word that has the number code **4534**.   NEON

/ 3

FOAL   LOAF   LATE   TEAL

5413   6213   3216

22. Find the code for the word **LATE**.   3154
23. Find the code for the word **TALL**.   5133
24. Find the word that has the number code **6315**.   FLEA

/ 3

Section Five — Logic and Coding

Explore the Facts

> Read the information carefully, then use it to answer the question that follows. Write your answer on the line.

Hint: Some questions contain lots of information — write it in a grid to help you answer the question.

1. Jane, Debbie, Victoria, Lisa and Pierre all enjoy horse riding.

   Everyone except Victoria rides on Saturday. Pierre rides after school on Monday. Only Lisa and Victoria ride on Sunday morning. Lisa also rides on Wednesday.

   Who goes riding **most** often? _____

2. Alice, Grace, Rana, Mark and William are all going on holiday this year.

   Grace and Rana are going on an activity holiday. Mark is going to Ireland. Alice is going to a hotel in France. Rana, Grace and Alice are going camping. William is going on a cycling holiday in Devon with Mark.

   Who is going on the **fewest** holidays? _____

3. Haj, Jason, Georgia, Rosie and Lucy all like pizza, especially with unusual toppings.

   Everyone likes raisins, except Jason and Lucy. Jason's favourite topping is baked beans. Georgia and Haj eat lemon curd on their pizza. Lucy and Haj both like sausages.

   Who likes the **most** toppings on their pizza? _____

4. James, Edward, Ellie, Shreena and Alec are talking about their plans for the weekend.

   James, Edward and Ellie are all going swimming. Shreena and Alec are visiting family. Ellie and Shreena plan to go to the cinema. The boys are going shopping. Everyone except Edward plans to go to the park.

   Who has the **fewest** plans for the weekend? _____

Explore the Facts

> Read the information carefully, then use it to answer the question that follows. Write your answer on the line.

5. Marta, Jafar, Oliver, Poppy and Neal are all going on school trips this year.

   Oliver and Neal are going to an art gallery. Poppy, Marta and Jafar are going to the science museum and also on school picnic. Oliver is going on a trip to France. Marta and Jafar are going to the theatre.

   Who is going to visit the **fewest** places? _____   / 1

6. Lee, Louise, Spencer, Emma and Kristina all had tests at school.

   Lee scored the highest in Maths. Emma scored the highest mark in Art. Kristina came top in French, but didn't do well in Maths. Spencer and Louise scored the highest marks in Science and Spencer was top in History.

   Who came top in the **most** subjects? _____   / 1

7. Katya, Juan, Hannah, Wayne and Julia all go to swimming club.

   Juan goes swimming every day apart from Tuesday. Hannah and Julia swim every Wednesday. Hannah also swims on Saturday with Wayne. Katya goes swimming with Wayne every Sunday and Monday.

   Who swims the **fewest** number of days per week? _____   / 1

8. Callum, Maddie, Geeta, Charlie and Lin all have pets.

   Four of them have a dog. Maddie is the only one who has a pony. Geeta and Charlie have a hamster each. Callum also has a hamster, but he doesn't have a dog. They all have a pet cat, apart from Geeta and Charlie.

   Who has the **most** pets? _____   / 1

Section Five — Logic and Coding

Solve the Riddle

Key Question: Read the information carefully, then use it to answer the question that follows. Underline the correct answer.

Hint: Remember your final answer <u>must</u> be true or false. Don't choose an answer that only <u>might</u> be true or false.

1. Max, Charlotte, Ahmed and Victoria all attend a running club. Max runs faster than Charlotte. Victoria runs faster than Max. Ahmed is slower than Charlotte.

   If these statements are true, only one of these sentences below **must** be true. Which one?

   A   Charlotte runs faster than Victoria.
   B   Max runs faster than Victoria.
   C   Ahmed is quicker than Victoria.
   D   Max is the fastest runner.
   E   Max runs faster than Ahmed.

2. Sophie, Karl, Daisy, Josh and Abbie are talking about their houses. Sophie lives in a house with three bedrooms. Karl and Daisy both live in houses with more bedrooms than Sophie's. Abbie's house doesn't have a garden. Josh's house has half as many bedrooms as Karl's.

   If these statements are true, only one of these sentences below **cannot** be true. Which one?

   A   Daisy lives in a house with four bedrooms.
   B   Abbie's house is semi-detached.
   C   Karl's house has five bedrooms.
   D   Daisy's house is bigger than Abbie's.
   E   Josh has his own bedroom.

3. Laura, Georgia, Rohan and Jamie were all born in August. Georgia was born before Laura, but after Jamie. Rohan was born after Jamie.

   If these statements are true, only one of these sentences below **must** be true. Which one?

   A   Laura is older than Georgia.
   B   Georgia was born on the same day as Rohan.
   C   Jamie was born after Georgia.
   D   Laura is older than Rohan.
   E   Jamie is the oldest.

Section Five — Logic and Coding

Solve the Riddle

Key Question: Read the information carefully, then use it to answer the question that follows. Underline the correct answer.

4. Last year, the average temperature in August was 2 degrees hotter than in June. The average temperature in June was 15 degrees Celsius — that was 7 degrees less than July's average. The coldest day in September was 8 degrees cooler than August's average.

   If these statements are true, only one of these sentences below **cannot** be true. Which one?

   A   Average temperature in July was 22 degrees Celsius.

   B   The coldest day in September was 9 degrees.

   C   July was hotter than June.

   D   July was cooler than August.

   E   September was cooler than August.

5. Patrick, Angharad, Hannah, Jacob and Sushmita all need to catch buses to meet in town. Jacob's bus arrives 15 minutes after Hannah's bus. Sushmita's bus arrives 20 minutes before Angharad's. Patrick's bus arrives at 7.15pm. Hannah's bus arrives 10 minutes after Patrick's.

   If these statements are true, only one of these sentences below **must** be true. Which one?

   A   Hannah's bus arrives at 7.30pm.

   B   Jacob's bus arrives at 7.40pm.

   C   Hannah lives further from town than Jacob.

   D   Patrick and Sushmita arrive at the same time.

   E   Sushmita arrives at 7.50pm.

6. Lily, Charlie, Grace, Lucy and Dan are given money to spend on attracting visitors to their school fair. Charlie spends more than £10. Together, Grace and Dan spend £20 on paint to design posters. Lucy buys four banners for £3 each. Dan's paint costs £6.50. Lily spends half as much as Lucy.

   If these statements are true, only one of these sentences below **must** be true. Which one?

   A   Charlie spends more than Grace.

   B   Grace spends less than Lucy.

   C   Dan spends the same amount as Grace.

   D   Grace spends more than Lily.

   E   Lucy spends the most money.

   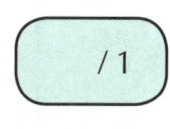

Section Five — Logic and Coding

Letter Connections

Key Question: Find the pair of letters that completes each sentence in the most sensible way. Use the alphabet to help you.

A B C D E F G H I J K L M N O P Q R S T U V W X Y Z

Look at this example:

AD is to **BE** as **MP** is to (NQ)

1. **CH** is to **EJ** as **LN** is to (NP)
2. **RU** is to **TW** as **FH** is to (HJ)
3. **GJ** is to **FI** as **OR** is to (NQ)
4. **FR** is to **JV** as **LS** is to (PW)
5. **AZ** is to **CX** as **BY** is to (DW)
6. **CB** is to **HG** as **NM** is to (SR)

7. **AD** is to **ZE** as **PR** is to (KS)
8. **YM** is to **AO** as **LF** is to (NH)
9. **JO** is to **LL** as **QY** is to (SV)
10. **SH** is to **VE** as **WD** is to (ZA)
11. **PS** is to **LR** as **BG** is to (XF)
12. **LO** is to **IR** as **RI** is to (OL)

13. **NU** is to **IP** as **DA** is to (YV)
14. **SL** is to **VI** as **RB** is to (UY)
15. **QJ** is to **MN** as **UF** is to (QJ)
16. **JV** is to **MW** as **FR** is to (IS)
17. **FP** is to **CR** as **LX** is to (IZ)
18. **TG** is to **YB** as **VE** is to (AZ)

Hint: The first and second letter in the pair don't always move in the same way, so make sure you work out the pattern for each of them.

Word Grids

Use the words to fill in the blanks in the word grids. You must use all the words. One letter for each grid has been filled in for you.

Hint: Cross out the words as you put them into the grid so you can see which ones are left.

1. might, eight, drive, dream

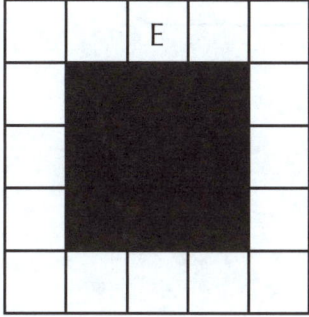

2. shine, lease, erase, shell

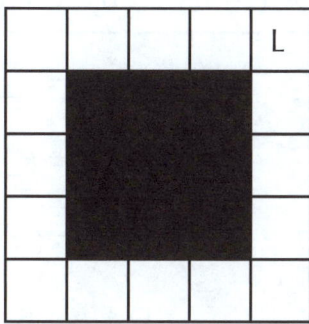

3. loyal, annoy, crave, sunny

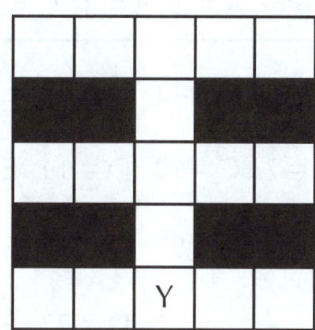

/ 3

4. under, ripen, terse, rapid

5. timid, local, mimic, tidal, admit

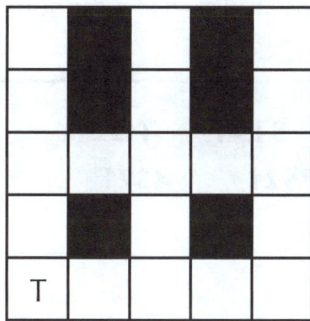

6. heart, armed, tombs, tests, hotly

/ 3

7. orate, blank, table, troop, poker

8. rivet, rocks, cease, treat, skirt

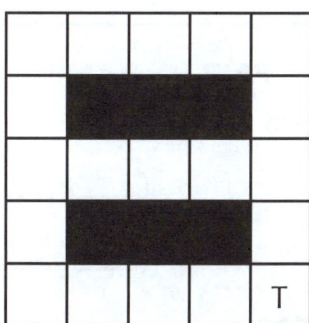

9. north, medic, mourn, donor, catch

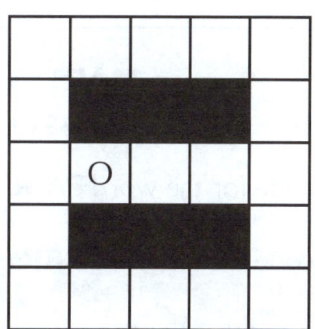

/ 3

Section Five — Logic and Coding

Assessment Test 1

The rest of the book contains seven assessment tests, which get progressively harder.

Allow 40 minutes to do each test and work as quickly and as carefully as you can.

If you want to attempt each test more than once, you will need to print **multiple-choice answer sheets** for these questions from our website — go to cgpbooks.co.uk/11plus/answer-sheets or scan the QR code on the right. If you'd prefer to answer them in standard write-in format, just follow the instructions in the question.

Answer Sheets

Each letter stands for a number. Work out the answer to each sum as a letter.

Example: A = 2 B = 3 C = 5 D = 9 E = 15   B × C = (__E__)

1. A = 3 B = 8 C = 13 D = 20 E = 24   A × B = (_____)

2. A = 2 B = 7 C = 10 D = 14 E = 24   D ÷ B = (_____)

3. A = 6 B = 7 C = 9   D = 18 E = 24   E − D = (_____)

4. A = 2 B = 6 C = 17 D = 22 E = 25   D ÷ A + B = (_____)

5. A = 1 B = 3 C = 5   D = 7   E = 18   E ÷ B − B = (_____)

/ 5

The number codes for three of these four words are listed in a random order. Work out the code to answer the questions.

TOYS   YOGA   STAY   TOGA
           6413   3521   4521

6. Find the code for the word **TOYS**.   (_____)

7. Find the code for the word **STAG**.   (_____)

8. Find the word that has the number code **2514**.   (_____)

/ 3

The number codes for three of these four words are listed in a random order. Work out the code to answer the questions.

MAIM   RAIN   PAIR   RAMP
           4512   4536   1531

9. Find the code for the word **PAIR**.   (_____)

10. Find the code for the word **PRIM**.   (_____)

11. Find the word that has the number code **2536**.   (_____)

/ 3

Assessment Test 1

In each sentence below, a four-letter word is hidden at the end of one word and the start of the next. **Either** mark the part of the sentence that contains the hidden word on the answer sheet, **or** write the hidden word on the line.

Example: Yesterday Fred broke thi<u>s hoe</u>. (__shoe__)

12. Josh edited his winning story. (_____)

13. Ayesha went walking with emus. (_____)

14. The cow entered the field. (_____)

15. We're having pizza for tea. (_____)

16. The silver urn is hot. (_____)

/ 5

Find the number that continues each sequence in the best way.

Example: 12, 12, 10, 10, 8, (__8__)

17. **7, 14, 14, 21, 21,** (_____)

18. **36, 30, 24, 18, 12,** (_____)

19. **5, 10, 20, 40,** (_____)

20. **50, 45, 40, 35, 30,** (_____)

21. **4, 5, 7, 10, 14,** (_____)

/ 5

Mark two words, one from each set of brackets, that have the most similar meaning.

Example: (young mother <u>old</u>)   (<u>elderly</u> new brother)

22. (big main ugly)   (small large cold)

23. (run camp wet)   (cold damp sleep)

24. (most small huge)   (little lots some)

25. (sad moan happy)   (angry yell glad)

26. (run mark push)   (walk sprint pull)

27. (pen sketch book)   (leaflet paint draw)

/ 6

Carry on to the next question → →

Assessment Test 1

28. Emma, Seren, Kate, Oisin and Tom are talking about how they travel to school.
Emma and Seren travel to school by bus every day. Kate and Oisin go by car each day apart from Tuesday. On Tuesday, they get the bus. Tom walks to school every day except Friday.

If these statements are true, only one of the sentences below **cannot** be true. Which one?

- **A** Kate goes to school by car on Monday.
- **B** Tom walks to school on Monday.
- **C** All the children go to school by bus on Tuesday.
- **D** Seren and Emma travel by bus on Wednesday.
- **E** Oison travels by car on Friday.

29. Oliver, Amaya, Katya, Timur and Rosie all go to bed at different times. Rosie goes before Katya but after Timur. Amaya and Oliver go to bed at the same time. Katya goes to bed before Oliver.

If these statements are true, only one of the sentences below **must** be true. Which one?

- **A** Katya goes to bed earliest.
- **B** Timur goes to bed after Rosie.
- **C** Rosie goes to bed at 8.30pm.
- **D** Amaya goes to bed after Rosie.
- **E** Oliver goes to bed after Amaya.

Find the pair of letters that completes each sentence in the most sensible way.
Use the alphabet to help you.

A B C D E F G H I J K L M N O P Q R S T U V W X Y Z

Example: **AB** is to **BC** as **DE** is to (__EF__).

30. **PX** is to **OW** as **MT** is to (LS).

31. **DW** is to **EV** as **GT** is to (HS).

32. **RV** is to **VZ** as **NQ** is to (RU).

33. **FJ** is to **FL** as **NP** is to (NR).

34. **MN** is to **JQ** as **JQ** is to (GT).

Mark two words, one from each set of brackets, that complete the sentence in the most sensible way.

Example: Train is to (carriage ticket <u>track</u>) as **car** is to (petrol wheel <u>road</u>).

35. **Hat** is to (hair head warm) as **glove** is to (hand foot winter).

36. **Car** is to (walk drive play) as **bike** is to (run ride fall).

37. **Sky** is to (blue cloud bird) as **grass** is to (grow mow green).

38. **Doctor** is to (brain hospital health) as **teacher** is to (book library school).

39. **Trunk** is to (bear deer elephant) as **antenna** is to (ant mole badger).

/ 5

The words in the second set follow the same pattern as the words in the first set. Find the missing word to complete the second set.

Example: pot (hot) how   tip (__sip__) sea

40. dog (get) met   pat (_____) mop

41. felt (ten) nail   mast (_____) grow

42. cart (not) honk   make (_____) scan

43. milk (lip) nape   dart (_____) same

44. nip (pig) peg   nag (_____) fit

45. mire (rim) fine   both (_____) make

/ 6

Find the number that completes the final set of numbers in the same way as the first two sets.

Example: 2 (5) 3   5 (7) 2   8 (__10__) 2

46. 1 (2) 1   2 (4) 2   3 (____) 3

47. 6 (9) 3   8 (14) 6   7 (____) 9

48. 4 (11) 15   9 (6) 15   6 (____) 18

49. 3 (6) 9   7 (10) 13   4 (____) 10

50. 6 (12) 2   3 (9) 3   4 (____) 8

/ 5

Carry on to the next question → →

Assessment Test 1

Mark the word outside the brackets that has a similar meaning to the words in both sets of brackets.

Example: (charge fee)   (sunny bright)   summer   cost   <u>fine</u>

51. (harden solidify)   (group type)   jelly   kind   set
52. (solid tough)   (difficult tricky) hard   easy   uneven
53. (see notice)   (pimple blackhead) look   spot   stain
54. (tin container)   (could able)   vessel   can   capable
55. (stick racket)   (knock strike)   bat   hurt   hit

/ 5

Find the letter that will finish the first word and start the second word of each pair. The same letter must be used for both pairs. **Either** mark the letter on the answer sheet, **or** write it on the line.

Example: car (?) ame   se (?) erm   (__t__)

56. bat (?) at   as (?) am   (_____)
57. ja (?) ost har (?) ake   (_____)
58. sto (?) od lea (?) it   (_____)
59. rot (?) nd se (?) pe   (_____)
60. sti (?) ail oa (?) at   (_____)

/ 5

Total / 60

End of Test

Assessment Test 1

Assessment Test 2

Allow 40 minutes to do this test. Work as quickly and as carefully as you can.

You can print **multiple-choice answer sheets** for these questions from our website — go to cgpbooks.co.uk/11plus/answer-sheets or scan the QR code on the right. If you'd prefer to answer them in standard write-in format, just follow the instructions in the question.

Read the information carefully, then use it to answer the question that follows.

1. Daneesh, Glenda, Jean, Taylor and Nadia like different things for breakfast. Everyone likes cereal except for Glenda. Daneesh and Taylor like yoghurt. Glenda and Jean like porridge. Daneesh, Glenda and Nadia like toast.

   Who likes the **most** things for breakfast?   (_____)

2. Tim, Georgia, Max, Charlotte and Callum all earn pocket money. Tim and Max spend theirs on sweets and football magazines. Charlotte buys sweets and music. Callum and Georgia buy clothes. Max and Georgia like to buy presents for their friends.

   Who buys the **most** things with their pocket money?   (_____)

   / 2

Find the pair of letters that continues each sequence in the best way.
Use the alphabet to help you.

A B C D E F G H I J K L M N O P Q R S T U V W X Y Z

Example: AA   BA   CA   DA   (<u>EA</u>)

3. LA   NB   PC   RD   (_____)
4. WZ   RU   MP   HK   (_____)
5. JM   IO   HQ   GS   (_____)
6. TX   QW   NV   KU   (_____)
7. TM   RO   PQ   NS   (_____)
8. AX   EU   IR   MO   (_____)

/ 6

Carry on to the next question → →

Assessment Test 2

Three of the words in each list are linked.
Mark the two words that are not related to these three.

Example: pen   pencil   <u>paper</u>   <u>card</u>   crayon

9. big   huge   mini   tiny   gigantic

10. fox   cat   dog   hamster   badger

11. nose   finger   eye   foot   mouth

12. earring   scarf   jumper   necklace   bracelet

13. apple   carrot   cabbage   cauliflower   strawberry

/ 5

Find the missing number to complete each sum.

Example: 10 + 5 = (__15__)

14. 18 ÷ 3 = (_____)

15. 21 − 8 = (_____)

16. 7 × 2 = (_____)

17. 12 × 2 − 2 = (_____)

18. 8 ÷ 2 + 12 = (_____)

/ 5

Find the three-letter word that completes the word in capital letters, and so finishes the sentence in a sensible way.

Example: I played **FOOTB** at the weekend.   (__ALL__)

19. We took buckets and **SES** with us to the beach.   (_____)

20. The four seasons are spring, summer, autumn and **TER**.   (_____)

21. I bought a new scarf when I went **SPING** in town.   (_____)

22. A **MERM** has the tail of a fish and the body of a woman.   (_____)

23. The film is **SING** at the cinema at 7pm.   (_____)

/ 5

Assessment Test 2

The number codes for three of these four words are listed in a random order.
Work out the code to answer the questions.

WHIP   WEIR   PIER   WIPE
4362   1534   1346

24. Find the code for the word **WHIP**.   (1534)

25. Find the code for the word **WIRE**.   (1326)

26. Find the word that has the number code **2346**.   (RIPE)

/ 3

The number codes for three of these four words are listed in a random order.
Work out the code to answer the questions.

SOUR   TEST   ROSE   SURE
4612   4561   3243

27. Find the code for the word **TEST**.   (3243)

28. Find the code for the word **RUST**.   (1643)

29. Find the word that has the number code **5614**.   (OURS)

/ 3

Mark a word from the first set, followed by a word from the second set, that go together to form a new word.

Example: (dog cat <u>cow</u>)   (man <u>boy</u> lad)   (the new word is 'cowboy')

30. (<u>sun</u> crowd car)   (wind <u>shine</u> dark)

31. (eve party <u>birth</u>)   (<u>day</u> song tomorrow)

32. (sky lit <u>air</u>)   (boot dock <u>port</u>)

33. (<u>eye</u> head nose)   (brim <u>brow</u> foot)

34. (<u>butter</u> cake pan)   (<u>fly</u> flour bowl)

35. (watch hour <u>clock</u>)   (<u>work</u> know second)

/ 6

Carry on to the next question → →

Assessment Test 2

Find the word that completes the third pair of words so that it follows the same pattern as the first two pairs.

Example: pants ant   toner one   harms (__arm__)

36. rabbit bit   unhand and   scrape (_____)
37. portal port   masses mass   camels (_____)
38. stamps map   starts rat   browns (_____)
39. places sap   trails sat   paired (_____)
40. parking pin   betrays bay   hallows (_____)

/ 5

Mark two words, one from each set of brackets, that have the most opposite meaning.

Example: (shiny <u>new</u> unused)   (<u>old</u> shabby dusty)

41. (sunrise sky dark)   (dawn night sunset)
42. (sad huge heavy)   (cry dense tiny)
43. (human boy woman)   (girl young child)
44. (pudding evening sleep)   (tea morning breakfast)
45. (summer month dry)   (warm harvest winter)

/ 5

Remove one letter from the first word and add it to the second word to make two new words. Do not change the order of the other letters. **Either** mark the letter that moves on the answer sheet, **or** write the two new words on the lines.

Example: spell   ink   (__sell__) (__pink__)

46. rider   cash   (_____) (_____)
47. train   car   (_____) (_____)
48. pants   toy   (_____) (_____)
49. trash   urn   (_____) (_____)
50. flood   ate   (_____) (_____)

/ 5

Assessment Test 2

Mark two words, one from each set of brackets, that have the most similar meaning.

Example: (young mother <u>old</u>)   (<u>elderly</u> new brother)

51. (beach wave certain)   (fish shore cliff)
52. (taste drink meal)   (fork menu lunch)
53. (ring rock gem)   (crown jewel gold)
54. (coat skirt trousers)   (jacket scarf socks)
55. (chew smile wink)   (grin frown laugh)

/ 5

Find the pair of letters that completes each sentence in the most sensible way.
Use the alphabet to help you.

A B C D E F G H I J K L M N O P Q R S T U V W X Y Z

Example: **AB** is to **BC** as **DE** is to (<u>EF</u>).

56. **XO** is to **UL** as **PK** is to (_____).
57. **LO** is to **MN** as **JQ** is to (_____).
58. **DW** is to **BY** as **HS** is to (_____).
59. **QM** is to **MO** as **TJ** is to (_____).
60. **CM** is to **EK** as **HT** is to (_____).

/ 5

Total / 60

End of Test

Assessment Test 2

Assessment Test 3

Allow 40 minutes to do this test. Work as quickly and as carefully as you can.

You can print **multiple-choice answer sheets** for these questions from our website — go to cgpbooks.co.uk/11plus/answer-sheets or scan the QR code on the right. If you'd prefer to answer them in standard write-in format, just follow the instructions in the question.

Mark the word outside the brackets that has a similar meaning to the words in both sets of brackets.

Example: (charge fee)   (sunny bright)   summer   cost   <u>fine</u>

1. (alter adjust)   (coins money)   adapt   pocket   change
2. (knock tap)   (hip-hop urban)   rap   music   throw
3. (sack dismiss)   (blaze flames)   expel   bring   fire
4. (look observe)   (clock timer)   watch   time   view
5. (skill ability)   (present parcel)   talent   gift   wrapping

/ 5

Each letter stands for a number. Work out the answer to each sum as a letter.

Example: $A = 2$ $B = 3$ $C = 5$ $D = 9$ $E = 15$ $B \times C = ($ __E__ $)$

6. $A = 2$ $B = 4$ $C = 5$ $D = 8$ $E = 10$ $C \times B \div A = ($ _____ $)$
7. $A = 2$ $B = 3$ $C = 9$ $D = 13$ $E = 25$ $B \times C - E = ($ _____ $)$
8. $A = 2$ $B = 5$ $C = 6$ $D = 20$ $E = 21$ $C + D - E = ($ _____ $)$
9. $A = 4$ $B = 5$ $C = 6$ $D = 9$ $E = 13$ $A + B + D - E = ($ _____ $)$
10. $A = 4$ $B = 6$ $C = 8$ $D = 10$ $E = 22$ $C \times A - D = ($ _____ $)$

/ 5

The number codes for three of these four words are listed in a random order. Work out the code to answer the questions.

TAXI   TEXT   NINE   EXIT
5432   6365   2143

11. Find the code for the word **TEXT**.   (_____)
12. Find the code for the word **NEAT**.   (_____)
13. Find the word that has the number code **6542**.   (_____)

/ 3

Assessment Test 3

The number codes for three of these four words are listed in a random order.
Work out the code to answer the questions.

BEND   DINT   TEEN   TIDE
4321   5162   4116

14. Find the code for the word **DINT**. (_____)

15. Find the code for the word **BITE**. (_____)

16. Find the word that has the number code **5362**. (_____)

/ 3

Find the pair of letters that continues each sequence in the best way.
Use the alphabet to help you.

A B C D E F G H I J K L M N O P Q R S T U V W X Y Z

Example: AA   BA   CA   DA   (__EA__)

17. JJ   IK   HL   GM   (_____)

18. XG   AE   BC   EA   (_____)

19. PH   NL   LP   JT   (_____)

20. QG   NJ   KI   HL   (_____)

21. JF   LC   NZ   PW   (_____)

/ 5

Each question uses a different code. Use the alphabet to help you work out the answer to each question.

A B C D E F G H I J K L M N O P Q R S T U V W X Y Z

Example: If the code for **FOUR** is **CLRO**, what is **CFSB** the code for? (__FIVE__)

22. If the code for **DRINK** is **FTKPM**, what is the code for **GLASS**? (_____)

23. If the code for **CAT** is **XZG**, what is **WLT** the code for? (_____)

24. If the code for **SNAIL** is **TMBHM**, what is **TGFKM** the code for? (_____)

25. If the code for **ELM** is **VON**, what is **LZP** the code for? (_____)

26. If the code for **STIFF** is **NVDHA**, what is **GQJRT** the code for? (_____)

27. If the code for **SNOW** is **SKOT**, what is **SIIM** the code for? (_____)

/ 5

Carry on to the next question → →

Assessment Test 3

Find the letter that will finish the first word and start the second word of each pair. The same letter must be used for both pairs. **Either** mark the letter on the answer sheet, **or** write it on the line.

Example: car (?) ame   se (?) erm   (__t__)

28. fil (?) ill   glu (?) oat   (_____)

29. to (?) ear   sa (?) es   (_____)

30. ti (?) ail   fu (?) ew   (_____)

31. ja (?) oy   so (?) at   (_____)

32. si (?) en   pe (?) rap   (_____)

/ 5

The words in the second set follow the same pattern as the words in the first set. Find the missing word to complete the second set.

Example: pot (hot) how   tip (__sip__) sea

33. gasp (par) rage   fish (_____) mope

34. pink (rip) wire   mist (_____) dear

35. last (fat) flak   moat (_____) gram

36. stop (met) mate   bade (_____) tile

37. lime (lap) pale   wren (_____) daze

/ 5

Find the number that continues each sequence in the best way.

Example: 12, 12, 10, 10, 8, (__8__)

38. **49, 42, 35, 28, 21, (_____)**

39. **3, 4, 7, 11, 18, (_____)**

40. **7, 15, 23, 31, 39, (_____)**

41. **6, 8, 12, 14, 18, (_____)**

42. **32, 16, 8, 4, 2, (_____)**

43. **2, 8, 6, 10, 10, 12, (_____)**

/ 6

Assessment Test 3

Read the information carefully, then use it to answer the question that follows.

44. Callum, Giuseppe, Tanay, Theo and Helga support different football teams. Callum's favourite team has won five matches so far this season. Helga's team has lost three, but won four matches. Theo's team has won two more matches than Callum's team, but two less than Giuseppe's team. Tanay's team has lost four matches this season.

   If these statements are true, only one of the sentences below **cannot** be true. Which one?

   A   Helga's team has lost fewer matches than Tanay's team.
   B   Giuseppe's team has won more matches than Helga's team.
   C   Giuseppe's team has won all its matches this season.
   D   Callum's team has won fewer matches than Theo's team.
   E   Helga's team has won more matches than Theo's team.

45. A, B, C, D and E are five trains. Train A is faster than train C, but slower than train B. Train D is faster than train A, but slower than train E.

   If these statements are true, only one of the sentences below **must** be true. Which one?

   A   Trains E and D travel at the same speed.
   B   Train C is faster than train A.
   C   Train C is slower than train D.
   D   Train D is faster than train B.
   E   Train A is faster than train E.

/ 2

In each sentence below a four-letter word is hidden at the end of one word and the start of the next. **Either** mark the part of the sentence that contains the hidden word on the answer sheet, **or** write the hidden word on the line.

   Example: Yesterday Fred broke thi<u>s hoe</u>.   (__shoe__)

46. Who opened the biscuit tin?   (_____)

47. Suzi finished all her broccoli.   (_____)

48. Alec rowed the wooden boat.   (_____)

49. Aluminium drinks cans are recyclable. (_____)

50. I know what Grandpa thinks.   (_____)

/ 5

Carry on to the next question → →

Mark two words, one from each set of brackets, that complete the sentence in the most sensible way.

Example: Train is to (carriage ticket <u>track</u>) as **car** is to (petrol wheel <u>road</u>).

51. **Boy** is to (young loud man) as **girl** is to (old mother woman).

52. **Ice** is to (drink cold winter) as **fire** is to (hot summer chestnuts).

53. **Shy** is to (happy sad timid) as **confident** is to (young assured big).

54. **Book** is to (library page park) as **food** is to (ground eat supermarket).

55. **Cow** is to (milk field herd) as **sheep** is to (flock dog graze).

/ 5

Mark two words, one from each set of brackets, that have the most opposite meaning.

Example: (shiny <u>new</u> unused)   (<u>old</u> shabby dusty)

56. (between far towards)   (front beyond near)

57. (pause go wait)   (try stop gone)

58. (cry water shout)   (whisper hear video)

59. (tall short slim)   (skinny young lofty)

60. (speak own teach)   (listen you word)

/ 5

Total / 60

End of Test

Assessment Test 3

Assessment Test 4

Allow 40 minutes to do this test. Work as quickly and as carefully as you can.

You can print **multiple-choice answer sheets** for these questions from our website — go to cgpbooks.co.uk/11plus/answer-sheets or scan the QR code on the right. If you'd prefer to answer them in standard write-in format, just follow the instructions in the question.

Remove one letter from the first word and add it to the second word to make two new words. Do not change the order of the other letters. **Either** mark the letter that moves on the answer sheet, **or** write the two new words on the lines.

Example: spell   ink   (__sell__) (__pink__)

1. brain   ark   (_____) (_____)
2. fared   are   (_____) (_____)
3. frame   ice   (_____) (_____)
4. blown   pat   (_____) (_____)
5. caper   pot   (_____) (_____)

/ 5

Find the missing number to complete each sum.

Example: $10 + 5 = (\_15\_)$

6. $17 - 12 = 10 - (\_\_\_\_)$
7. $6 + 6 = 4 \times (\_\_\_\_)$
8. $19 + 2 = 3 \times (\_\_\_\_)$
9. $1 + 22 = 25 - (\_\_\_\_)$
10. $7 \times 4 = 2 \times (\_\_\_\_)$

/ 5

The number codes for three of these four words are listed in a random order. Work out the code to answer the questions.

FAKE   LACK   KALE   FLEA
1234   1642   6253

11. Find the code for the word **KALE**. (_____)
12. Find the code for the word **KEEL**. (_____)
13. Find the word that has the number code **5214**. (_____)

/ 3

Carry on to the next question → →

HOST   SHIN   TOSH   HINT
2136   1425   1365

14. Find the code for the word **TOSH**. (5421)

15. Find the code for the word **NITS**. (6352)

16. Find the word that has the number code **5132**. (THIS)

Three of the words in each list are linked.
Mark the two words that are not related to these three.

Example: pen   pencil   <u>paper</u>   <u>card</u>   crayon

17. <u>work</u>   <u>think</u>   sing   shout   chat

18. kitchen   <u>garden</u>   <u>garage</u>   bedroom   study

19. cup   glass   <u>plate</u>   <u>spoon</u>   beaker

20. <u>badminton</u>   netball   <u>tennis</u>   football   basketball

21. hail   <u>steam</u>   <u>air</u>   rain   snow

22. <u>man</u>   girl   boy   <u>lady</u>   child

23. Charlotte, Nikhil, Hannah, Carlos and Jamie all do different activities. Charlotte and Nikhil go to French Club after school on Monday. Hannah goes horseriding on Saturday morning with Carlos and Jamie. Jamie and Nikhil go swimming every Sunday. Hannah and Charlotte go to netball on Tuesday. Hannah goes swimming straight after that.

Who does the **fewest** activities? (Carlos)

24. Tom, Arushi, Lily, Abdul and Elsie all use mobile phones. They all use them for texting, except Arushi. Abdul, Lily and Tom use their phones to call friends. Elsie isn't allowed to use hers to make calls. Arushi and Abdul play games on their phones.

Who does the **most** things on their phone? (Abdul)

Mark a word from the first set, followed by a word from the second set, that go together to form a new word.

Example: (dog cat <u>cow</u>)   (man <u>boy</u> lad)   (the new word is 'cowboy')

25. (sheep lamb cow)   (dog cat pig)
26. (bang pop lemon)   (aid corn drink)
27. (picture camera photo)   (chart frame graph)
28. (great grand big)   (brother father sister)
29. (red birthday stair)   (case card carpet)

/ 5

Find the number that completes the final set of numbers in the same way as the first two sets.

Example: 2 (5) 3   5 (7) 2   8 (_10_) 2

30. 6 (18) 12   15 (25) 10   8 (_____) 4
31. 8 (5) 3   12 (5) 7   15 (_____) 12
32. 8 (10) 12   7 (11) 15   9 (_____) 15
33. 4 (24) 6   7 (21) 3   3 (_____) 5
34. 17 (10) 3   12 (9) 6   11 (_____) 7

/ 5

Find the three-letter word that completes the word in capital letters, and so finishes the sentence in a sensible way.

Example: I played **FOOTB** at the weekend.   (_ALL_)

35. I rang my mum on the **TELEPH** to say I would be late home.   (_____)
36. The audience **CPED** loudly when the play finished.   (_____)
37. It was a hot day so I had a **DR** of water.   (_____)
38. I am inviting 20 friends to my birthday **PY**.   (_____)
39. The astronaut went into **SP** in a rocket.   (_____)

/ 5

Carry on to the next question → →

Assessment Test 4

> Mark two words, one from each set of brackets, that have the most similar meaning.
>
> **Example:** (young mother <u>old</u>)   (<u>elderly</u> new brother)

40. (ignore curious clock) (interested inform look)

41. (excited loud tired) (angry drowsy yawn)

42. (cup fork eat) (plate dinner mug)

43. (bizarre funny boring) (alarmed tedious usual)

44. (employ chore faster) (task slower lazy)

45. (think forget worry) (remember concern horror)

/ 6

> Find the number that continues each sequence in the best way.
>
> **Example: 12, 12, 10, 10, 8, (_8_)**

46. **4, 11, 18, 25, 32,** (_____)

47. **2, 4, 8, 16, 32,** (_____)

48. **53, 44, 35, 26, 17,** (_____)

49. **10, 12, 20, 24, 30, 36,** (_____)

50. **16, 18, 22, 28, 36,** (_____)

/ 5

> Each question uses a different code. Use the alphabet to help you work out the answer to each question.
>
> A B C D E F G H I J K L M N O P Q R S T U V W X Y Z
>
> **Example:** If the code for **FOUR** is **CLRO**, what is **CFSB** the code for? (__FIVE__)

51. If the code for **SOCK** is **QLAH**, what is the code for **PINT**?   (_____)

52. If the code for **FADE** is **UZWV**, what is **SVZW** the code for?   (_____)

53. If the code for **WITCH** is **TNQHE**, what is **PUBQI** the code for?   (_____)

54. If the code for **TRAP** is **GIZK**, what is **DZHS** the code for?   (_____)

55. If the code for **BEST** is **WJNY**, what is the code for **MINT**?   (_____)

/ 5

Assessment Test 4

Find the word that completes the third pair of words so that it follows the same pattern as the first two pairs.

Example: pants ant   toner one   harms (__arm__)

56. dreamt ream   charms harm   tablet (_____)

57. planet pat   scared sad   closed (_____)

58. palace lap   muscle sum   nipper (_____)

59. priced dice   chalet tale   trails (_____)

60. marine mine   coward card   facade (_____)

/ 5

Total / 60

End of Test

Assessment Test 4

Assessment Test 5

Allow 40 minutes to do this test. Work as quickly and as carefully as you can.

You can print **multiple-choice answer sheets** for these questions from our website — go to cgpbooks.co.uk/11plus/answer-sheets or scan the QR code on the right. If you'd prefer to answer them in standard write-in format, just follow the instructions in the question.

Read the information carefully, then use it to answer the question that follows.

1. Poppy, Henry, Luke, Anna and Tara are watching different television programmes. Henry's programme started at 7.30pm and lasts for 90 minutes. Luke's programme started 30 minutes after Henry's. Anna and Poppy both start watching TV at 7.15pm. Tara's programme ends at 9.30pm, which is 20 minutes after Poppy's programme ends.

   If these statements are true, only one of the sentences below **cannot** be true. Which one?

   A   Tara sometimes watches television.
   B   Poppy's programme ends at 9.10pm.
   C   Luke's programme started at 8.10pm.
   D   Henry's TV programme ends at 9.00pm.
   E   Henry's programme lasts for longer than Luke's.

2. Jo, Theo, Rosie, Alex and Ben are siblings. Jo is 2 years older than Theo. Rosie is 4 years younger than Theo but 1 year older than Alex. Alex is 2 years old. Ben is the same age as Jo.

   If these statements are true, only one of the sentences below **cannot** be true. Which one?

   A   Ben was born before Theo.
   B   Jo and Ben are twins.
   C   Rosie is 6 years younger than Jo.
   D   Theo is 8 years old.
   E   Alex is 1 year younger than Rosie.

The number codes for three of these four words are listed in a random order. Work out the code to answer the questions.

WANE   DOWN   DEAD   NODE
5316   1264   5425

3. Find the code for the word **NODE**.   (_____)

4. Find the code for the word **WOOD**.   (_____)

5. Find the word that has the number code **6436**.   (_____)

The number codes for three of these four words are listed in a random order.
Work out the code to answer the questions.

SLAY   SOYA   BOYS   SLOB
4526   6523   6132

6. Find the code for the word **SLOB**. (_____)

7. Find the code for the word **SAYS**. (_____)

8. Find the word that has the number code **4566**. (_____)

/ 3

The words in the second set follow the same pattern as the words in the first set.
Find the missing word to complete the second set.

Example: pot (hot) how   tip (_sip_) sea

9. ripe (pin) pint   isle (_____) find

10. pace (cap) pass   fame (_____) pink

11. mine (men) nest   dims (_____) need

12. salt (sat) talk   doll (_____) trot

13. fork (tore) rote   sink (_____) cope

/ 5

Find the pair of letters that continues each sequence in the best way.
Use the alphabet to help you.

A B C D E F G H I J K L M N O P Q R S T U V W X Y Z

Example: AA   BA   CA   DA   (_EA_)

14. SE   VG   YI   BK   (_____)

15. YJ   VH   SD   PB   (_____)

16. WD   ZA   CX   FU   (_____)

17. KP   MQ   PR   RS   (_____)

18. HC   IE   KD   NF   (_____)

/ 5

Carry on to the next question → →

Assessment Test 5

Find the letter that will finish the first word and start the second word of each pair. The same letter must be used for both pairs. **Either** mark the letter on the answer sheet, **or** write it on the line.

Example: car (?) ame   se (?) erm   (__t__)

19. cal (?) it   loa (?) un   (_____)
20. ma (?) rim   roo (?) ap   (_____)
21. ru (?) ut   slu (?) as   (_____)
22. plu (?) ip   bu (?) and   (_____)
23. ni (?) ead   so (?) all   (_____)

/ 5

Mark two words, one from each set of brackets, that complete the sentence in the most sensible way.

Example: Train is to (carriage ticket <u>track</u>) as **car** is to (petrol wheel <u>road</u>).

24. **Gold** is to (picture sun jewellery) as **glass** is to (floor window water).
25. **Desert** is to (camel abandon sand) as **arctic** is to (ice cold holiday).
26. **Vast** is to (massive small quiet) as **tiny** is to (quick slim minute).
27. **Win** is to (first dart success) as **lose** is to (sad failure slow).
28. **Lamb** is to (chop sheep spring) as **calf** is to (cow pork winter).
29. **Rain** is to (drop umbrella cloud) as **snow** is to (storm drift flake).

/ 6

Each letter stands for a number. Work out the answer to each sum as a letter.

Example: A = 2 B = 3 C = 5 D = 9 E = 15   B × C = (__E__)

30. A = 4   B = 5   C = 9   D = 16   E = 24   A × B − A = (_____)
31. A = 4   B = 6   C = 20   D = 28   E = 32   B × A − C = (_____)
32. A = 1   B = 3   C = 8   D = 11   E = 16   E ÷ C − A = (_____)
33. A = 2   B = 5   C = 10   D = 13   E = 25   E ÷ B + C − A = (_____)
34. A = 2   B = 4   C = 7   D = 14   E = 21   E ÷ C × A − A = (_____)

/ 5

Assessment Test 5

Find the three-letter word that completes the word in capital letters, and so finishes the sentence in a sensible way.

Example: I played **FOOTB** at the weekend. (__ALL__)

35. The Duchess rode in a **CARRI** that was pulled by two horses. (AGE)
36. The brave **SIER** returned from war. (OLD)
37. The chef used lots of herbs and **SPS** to make the food taste good. (ICE)
38. My pancake stuck to the ceiling when I was **FLIPG** it. (PIN)
39. The children's **FAMIS** came to watch them in the concert. (LIE)

/ 5

In these questions the numbers in each group are related in the same way.

Find the missing number.

Example: 2 (5) 3   5 (7) 2   8 (__10__) 2

40. 7 (12) 17   4 (12) 20   10 (15) 20
41. 5 (15) 3   6 (30) 5   12 (48) 4
42. 5 (10) 20   6 (12) 24   4 (8) 16
43. 15 (5) 3   24 (2) 12   18 (3) 6
44. 5 (4) 2   12 (7) 6   9 (7) 3
45. 7 (16) 1   2 (8) 2   3 (20) 7

/ 6

Mark two words, one from each set of brackets, that have the most similar meaning.

Example: (young mother <u>old</u>)   (<u>elderly</u> new brother)

46. (acquire expire inspire)   (relieve motivate attend)
47. (residue cost remind)   (forget tedium debris)
48. (lack plenty poverty)   (enough abundance generous)
49. (answer repeat react)   (question agree reply)
50. (search run chase)   (find pursue meet)

/ 5

Carry on to the next question → →

Assessment Test 5

51. over — board
52. beet — root
53. day — light
54. how — ever
55. hay — wire

56. OP
57. AZ
58. ML
59. HW
60. QJ

Assessment Test 6

Allow 40 minutes to do this test. Work as quickly and as carefully as you can.

You can print **multiple-choice answer sheets** for these questions from our website — go to cgpbooks.co.uk/11plus/answer-sheets or scan the QR code on the right. If you'd prefer to answer them in standard write-in format, just follow the instructions in the question.

Read the information carefully, then use it to answer the question that follows.

1. Mark, Lucy, Molly, Alice and Declan all have plans for the future. Alice, Mark and Lucy would all like to live abroad. Everyone apart from Alice hopes to go to university. Declan and Molly plan to be teachers. Lucy and Alice want to work with animals. Molly, Declan and Alice are all thinking of learning a foreign language.

    Who has the **fewest** plans for the future?   (_____)

2. Jenni, Becky, Edward, Rafi and Luke all like ice cream. Everyone apart from Edward likes vanilla. Rafi and Becky like strawberry. Jenni likes chocolate and she also likes mint. Edward and Luke like coffee flavour, but not strawberry.

    Who likes the **most** flavours of ice cream?   (_____)

Find the number that continues each sequence in the best way.

    Example: 12, 12, 10, 10, 8, (_8_)

3. **47, 39, 31, 23, (_____)**

4. **3, 10, 6, 15, 12, 20, (_____)**

5. **2, 8, 24, 48, (_____)**

6. **9, 10, 12, 15, 19, (_____)**

7. **4, 5, 9, 14, 23, (_____)**

Carry on to the next question → →

In each sentence below a four-letter word is hidden at the end of one word and the start of the next. **Either** mark the part of the sentence that contains the hidden word on the answer sheet, **or** write the hidden word on the line.

Example: Yesterday Fred broke this hoe. (__shoe__)

8. Steph ate her green cabbage quickly. (_____)

9. This year nobody skied in France. (_____)

10. We are going to the park. (_____)

11. Janet chose steak at the café. (_____)

12. They taught yoga in small groups. (_____)

/ 5

Find the letter that will finish the first word and start the second word of each pair. The same letter must be used for both pairs. **Either** mark the letter on the answer sheet, **or** write it on the line.

Example: car (?) ame   se (?) erm   (__t__)

13. sin (?) een   ar (?) ick   (_____)

14. le (?) ock   thu (?) ale   (_____)

15. dis (?) ove   tal (?) ap   (_____)

16. cro (?) ell   fla (?) ag   (_____)

17. gri (?) ool   li (?) ain   (_____)

/ 5

Mark two words, one from each set of brackets, that have the most opposite meaning.

Example: (shiny new unused)   (old shabby dusty)

18. (lose race trophy)   (medal second win)

19. (beside above next)   (down below inside)

20. (offer borrow deliver)   (bring lend post)

21. (selfish thoughtless rude) (popular generous greedy)

22. (museum antique relic)   (modern ancient remains)

/ 5

Assessment Test 6

The number codes for three of these four words are listed in a random order.
Work out the code to answer the questions.

ALOE   DOVE   DEAL   OVAL
3265   1465   6534

23. Find the code for the word **DOVE**. (_____)

24. Find the code for the word **VOLE**. (_____)

25. Find the word that has the number code **5461**. (_____)

/ 3

The number codes for three of these four words are listed in a random order.
Work out the code to answer the questions.

COPE   LOCK   POKE   PECK
3246   4215   1546

26. Find the code for the word **POKE**. (_____)

27. Find the code for the word **LEEK**. (_____)

28. Find the word that has the number code **3215**. (_____)

/ 3

Mark the word outside the brackets that has a similar meaning to the words in both sets of brackets.

Example: (charge fee)   (sunny bright)   summer   cost   <u>fine</u>

29. (holiday voyage)   (fall stumble)   tour   plunge   trip

30. (period time)   (magic incantation) stretch   spell   charm

31. (tiny miniature)   (moment instant)   small   clock   minute

32. (hurried quick)   (abstain diet)   fast   hasty   slim

33. (empty void)   (cave dip)   free   hollow   cavern

34. (shape sculpt)   (decay rot)   mould   whittle   spoil

/ 6

Carry on to the next question → →

Assessment Test 6

Remove one letter from the first word and add it to the second word to make two new words. Do not change the order of the other letters. **Either** mark the letter that moves on the answer sheet, **or** write the two new words on the lines.

Example: spell   ink   (__sell__) (__pink__)

35. miner   cat   (_____) (_____)

36. crash   rib   (_____) (_____)

37. float   son   (_____) (_____)

38. bread   bow   (_____) (_____)

39. piper   act   (_____) (_____)

/ 5

Find the word that completes the third pair of words so that it follows the same pattern as the first two pairs.

Example: pants ant   toner one   harms (__arm__)

40. bustle tub   guides dug   damson (_____)

41. fenced fed   pillar par   piglet (_____)

42. sweet wet   lapse ape   tangy (_____)

43. cheese she   papers rap   bottle (_____)

44. beaker rake   heaven nave   daring (_____)

/ 5

In these questions the numbers in each group are related in the same way. Find the missing number.

Example: 2 (5) 3   5 (7) 2   8 (__10__) 2

45. 3 (24) 8   9 (45) 5   8 (_____) 4

46. 2 (5) 10   7 (2) 14   6 (_____) 18

47. 4 (14) 15   8 (7) 12   6 (_____) 20

48. 5 (18) 4   2 (16) 6   7 (_____) 3

49. 6 (4) 3   8 (7) 2   4 (_____) 1

/ 5

Assessment Test 6

Find the missing number to complete each sum.

Example: 10 + 5 = (__15__)

50. 4 × 6 + 5 = (_____)

51. 17 – 8 + 15 = (_____)

52. 10 × 2 – 4 = 25 – (_____)

53. 18 ÷ 6 × 2 = 12 ÷ (_____)

54. 3 × 3 + 9 = (_____) + 6

55. 6 × 4 – 9 = (_____) – 2

/ 5

Each question uses a different code. Use the alphabet to help you work out the answer to each question.

A B C D E F G H I J K L M N O P Q R S T U V W X Y Z

Example: If the code for **FOUR** is **CLRO**, what is **CFSB** the code for? (__FIVE__)

56. If the code for **SHAPE** is **SICSI**, what is the code for **MUSIC**? (_____)

57. If the code for **HOUSE** is **FNUTG**, what is **AKODM** the code for? (_____)

58. If the code for **SQUID** is **ROREY**, what is the code for **SNOUT**? (_____)

59. If the code for **FIELD** is **URVOW**, what is **HSVVK** the code for? (_____)

60. If the code for **CREAM** is **XIVZN**, what is **DSRHP** the code for? (_____)

/ 5

Total / 60

End of Test

Assessment Test 6

Assessment Test 7

Allow 40 minutes to do this test. Work as quickly and as carefully as you can.

You can print **multiple-choice answer sheets** for these questions from our website — go to cgpbooks.co.uk/11plus/answer-sheets or scan the QR code on the right. If you'd prefer to answer them in standard write-in format, just follow the instructions in the question.

Find the missing number to complete each sum.

Example: 10 + 5 = (__15__)

1. 24 ÷ 2 − 2 = (_____) − 8
2. 7 × 4 + 4 = 25 + (_____)
3. 12 × 2 − 16 = 4 × (_____)
4. 2 × 8 ÷ 4 = 9 − (_____)
5. 20 ÷ 4 × 3 = 9 + (_____)

/ 5

Mark two words, one from each set of brackets, that have the most opposite meaning.

Example: (shiny <u>new</u> unused)   (<u>old</u> shabby dusty)

6. (deserted hermit alone)   (stranger separate together)
7. (early time lazy)   (keen watch delayed)
8. (happy sulk smile)   (frown laugh grin)
9. (rain cloud windy)   (rainbow mist still)
10. (awake arise tired)   (asleep drowsy snore)

/ 5

Each letter stands for a number. Work out the answer to each sum as a letter.

Example: A = 2 B = 3 C = 5 D = 9 E = 15   B × C = (__E__)

11. A = 1 B = 3 C = 5   D = 6   E = 13   C × B − E + B = (_____)
12. A = 2 B = 4 C = 9   D = 21 E = 25   E × A − E − B = (_____)
13. A = 3 B = 7 C = 10 D = 14 E = 21   E − C + A + B = (_____)
14. A = 3 B = 4 C = 6   D = 16 E = 18   E ÷ C × B + B = (_____)
15. A = 2 B = 4 C = 8   D = 12 E = 24   E ÷ C × B − C = (_____)

/ 5

Find the three-letter word that completes the word in capital letters, and so finishes the sentence in a sensible way.

Example: I played **FOOTB** at the weekend. (__ALL__)

16. I **PED** gravy on my roast dinner. (_____)

17. The **ADCED** maths questions were very difficult. (_____)

18. The **FORY** that made clothes had three large chimneys. (_____)

19. The crocodile **SPED** its jaws shut. (_____)

20. Sleeping Beauty pricked her finger on a **SNING** wheel. (_____)

21. We learn about **GMAR** in English lessons. (_____)

/ 6

Three of the words in each list are linked.
Mark the two words that are not related to these three.

Example: pen   pencil   paper   card   crayon

22. lake   pond   river   stream   reservoir

23. mouse   television   monitor   stereo   keyboard

24. wellingtons   anorak   shawl   umbrella   fan

25. limerick   hymn   lullaby   sonnet   haiku

26. England   France   India   Spain   China

/ 5

Find the pair of letters that continues each sequence in the best way.
Use the alphabet to help you.

A B C D E F G H I J K L M N O P Q R S T U V W X Y Z

Example: AA   BA   CA   DA   (__EA__)

27. WM   BP   GS   LV   (_____)

28. FG   EE   EF   FD   HE   (_____)

29. PB   KF   FD   AH   (_____)

30. JM   KM   MN   PP   (_____)

31. DX   EW   GU   HT   (_____)

/ 5

Carry on to the next question → →

Assessment Test 7

Remove one letter from the first word and add it to the second word to make two new words. Do not change the order of the other letters. **Either** mark the letter that moves on the answer sheet, **or** write the two new words on the lines.

Example: spell   ink   (__sell__) (__pink__)

32. trust   ore   (_____) (_____)

33. brush   fen   (_____) (_____)

34. cloth   sell   (_____) (_____)

35. draft   dew   (_____) (_____)

36. stomp   cob   (_____) (_____)

/ 5

Mark two words, one from each set of brackets, that complete the sentence in the most sensible way.

Example: Train is to (carriage ticket <u>track</u>) as **car** is to (petrol wheel <u>road</u>).

37. **Alarm** is to (shock morning jump) as **peace** is to (cheery fear calmness).

38. **Freedom** is to (open space liberty) as **captivity** is to (prison confinement fear).

39. **Truth** is to (good honesty free) as **lie** is to (recline sincere deception).

40. **Stall** is to (car market stop) as **advance** is to (go loan forward).

41. **Today** is to (past present tomorrow) as **yesterday** is to (today after future).

/ 5

The number codes for three of these four words are listed in a random order. Work out the code to answer the questions.

RIOT   FOIL   TOIL   FLIT
2346   5431   5136

42. Find the code for the word **TOIL**.   (_____)

43. Find the code for the word **LOOT**.   (_____)

44. Find the word that has the number code **1356**.   (_____)

/ 3

Assessment Test 7

The number codes for three of these four words are listed in a random order.
Work out the code to answer the questions.

EELS   USED   DEAL   DUEL
2653   3251   3541

45. Find the code for the word **EELS**.   (_____)

46. Find the code for the word **LEAD**.   (_____)

47. Find the word that has the number code **6541**.   (_____)

/ 3

Read the information carefully, then use it to answer the question that follows.

48. Alice, Ellie, Fryderyk, Ben and Sam all take part in a sponsored silence to raise money for charity. Ellie is silent for 20 minutes. Fryderyk and Sam are both silent for 5 minutes longer than Alice. Ben is silent for 28 minutes. Alice is silent for 4 minutes less than Ellie.

    If these statements are true, only one of the sentences below **cannot** be true. Which one?

    A   Ben is silent for the longest time.
    B   Fryderyk is silent for 21 minutes.
    C   Sam is silent for 7 minutes less than Ben.
    D   Ellie is silent for longer than Sam.
    E   All the children are silent for at least 15 minutes.

49. Almsbury, Batston, Corford, Drate and Elming are towns. Four of these towns have a theatre. All the towns have a bus station. Corford has a railway station, but no theatre. Drate has a hospital, a library and a cinema. Elming is the only town to have a sports centre as well as a theatre.

    If these statements are true, only one of the sentences below **must** be true. Which one?

    A   Only one town does not have a cinema.
    B   Drate and Corford both have hospitals.
    C   Almsbury doesn't have a bus station.
    D   Three towns have a railway station.
    E   Batston doesn't have a sports centre.

/ 2

Carry on to the next question → →

Assessment Test 7

Find the word that completes the third pair of words so that it follows the same pattern as the first two pairs.

Example: pants ant   toner one   harms (__arm__)

50. heaped pea   dancer can   hatred (__rat__)
51. before foe   empire pie   moaned (__and__)
52. iciest ice   cuddle dud   earwig (__raw__)
53. playpen plea perplex leer retinas (__neat__)
54. tomato toot   revive veer   dawdle (__lead__)

/ 5

Find the pair of letters that completes each sentence in the most sensible way. Use the alphabet to help you.

A B C D E F G H I J K L M N O P Q R S T U V W X Y Z

Example: **AB** is to **BC** as **DE** is to (__EF__).

55. **HP** is to **EU** as **BN** is to (__YS__).
56. **SZ** is to **WW** as **XT** is to (__BQ__).
57. **JB** is to **FD** as **BJ** is to (__XL__).
58. **XC** is to **VE** as **HS** is to (__FU__).
59. **MN** is to **IP** as **AY** is to (__WA__).
60. **KP** is to **NM** as **MN** is to (__PK__).

/ 6

Total / 60

End of Test

Answers

Page 2 — Alphabet Positions

1) **C** — C is at position 3 in the alphabet.
2) **X** — X is at position 24 in the alphabet.
3) **Z** — Z would be at position 1.
4) **O** — O would be at position 12.
5) **7** — G is at position 7 in the alphabet.
6) **8** — H is at position 8 in the alphabet.
7) **25** — Y is at position 25 in the alphabet.
8) **20** — T is at position 20 in the alphabet.
9) **D** — D would be at position 3.
10) **20** — Y would be at position 20.
11) **M** — M would be at position 10.
12) **7** — J would be at position 7.

Page 3 — Identify A Letter From A Clue

1) **B** — B is the only letter that occurs three times in HUBBUB.
2) **A** — A occurs most often in AVALANCHE.
3) **E** — E occurs most often in PREDECESSOR.
4) **A** — A occurs twice in ABANDON and three times in AARDVARK.
5) **I** — I occurs most often in INDIVIDUAL.
6) **C** — C occurs twice in ACCIDENT and twice in SPECIFIC.
7) **R** — R occurs once in SLOBBER and twice in RARITY.
8) **L** — L occurs once in POODLE and twice in LENTIL.
9) **E** — E occurs twice in LECTURER and twice in LESSER.
10) **R** — R occurs twice in ARRANGE and twice in TOMORROW.
11) **R** — R occurs twice in TERRAPIN, twice in RARIFY and twice in HORRIBLE.
12) **N** — N occurs three times in INNOCENT, twice in NOMINATE and twice in SNOWMAN.
13) **E** — E occurs twice in KERFUFFLE, three times in VENERABLE and twice in ELECTRIC.
14) **U** — U occurs twice in RUMPUS, twice in TRUCULENT and twice in UNANIMOUS.

Page 4 — Alphabetical Order

1) **sneak** — The words go in the order: 'sandy', 'slips', 'sneak', 'soapy', 'strap'.
2) **bless** — The words go in the order: 'beard', 'birth', 'bless', 'brown', 'bulls'.
3) **drops** — The words go in the order: 'drain', 'drape', 'dream', 'drops', 'drown'.
4) **floats** — The words go in the order: 'flames', 'flapper', 'flipper', 'floats', 'flower'.
5) **Y** — Y is the letter that comes last in the alphabet.
6) **E** — E is the letter that comes first in the alphabet.
7) **T** — T is the letter that comes last in the alphabet.
8) **E** — E is the letter that comes first in the alphabet.
9) **dreamer** — The words go in the order: 'calendar', 'dreamer', 'player', 'tremor', 'humour'.
10) **stretchy** — The words go in the order: 'biology', 'stretchy', 'happily', 'calmly', 'chemistry'.
11) **glowing** — The words go in the order: 'grinning', 'drawing', 'glowing', 'playing', 'snoozing'.
12) **spillage** — The words go in the order: 'cabbage', 'carriage', 'spillage', 'damage', 'dressage'.

Page 5 — Missing Letters

1) **z** — The new words are 'jazz', 'zoo', 'fizz' and 'zip'.
2) **e** — The new words are 'hope', 'earl', 'face' and 'eat'.
3) **o** — The new words are 'two', 'off', 'too' and 'one'.
4) **k** — The new words are 'bank', 'kite', 'hook' and 'king'.
5) **d** — The new words are 'find', 'drop', 'pad' and 'dot'.
6) **k** — The new words are 'ask', 'kid', 'book' and 'key'.
7) **l** — The new words are 'tall', 'lit', 'sill' and 'love'.
8) **g** — The new words are 'pig', 'glue', 'clog' and 'good'.
9) **e** — The new words are 'toe', 'ever', 'pie' and 'ear'.
10) **p** — The new words are 'map', 'pant', 'lap' and 'put'.
11) **h** — The new words are 'bush', 'hope', 'sash' and 'hot'.
12) **l** — The new words are 'meal', 'lose', 'pill' and 'law'.
13) **w** — The new words are 'saw', 'way', 'jaw' and 'won'.
14) **n** — The new words are 'bun', 'now', 'pin' and 'nice'.
15) **y** — The new words are 'easy', 'yard', 'pay' and 'yawn'.
16) **t** — The new words are 'sit', 'tag', 'cart' and 'tale'.
17) **w** — The new words are 'paw', 'win', 'sew' and 'wet'.
18) **e** — The new words are 'see', 'earn', 'mile' and 'ewe'.

Page 6 — Move A Letter

1) **w** — The new words are 'art' and 'warm'.
2) **d** — The new words are 'fin' and 'din'.
3) **m** — The new words are 'zoo' and 'mate'.
4) **b** — The new words are 'lame' and 'bore'.
5) **d** — The new words are 'one' and 'dwell'.
6) **f** — The new words are 'ace' and 'scarf'.
7) **f** — The new words are 'able' and 'fail'.
8) **r** — The new words are 'had' and 'rare'.
9) **o** — The new words are 'pen' and 'point'.
10) **f** — The new words are 'rat' and 'fact'.
11) **t** — The new words are 'ease' and 'stop'.
12) **b** — The new words are 'ring' and 'table'.
13) **r** — The new words are 'pot' and 'rate'.
14) **p** — The new words are 'soil' and 'park'.
15) **s** — The new words are 'cat' and 'silk'.
16) **m** — The new words are 'able' and 'time'.
17) **r** — The new words are 'cave' and 'roar'.
18) **r** — The new words are 'tan' and 'prop'.

Page 7 — Hidden Word

1) **best hat** — The hidden word is 'that'.
2) **time at** — The hidden word is 'meat'.
3) **No seats** — The hidden word is 'nose'.
4) **Sea monsters** — The hidden word is 'seam'.
5) **swam ashore** — The hidden word is 'mash'.
6) **Ted after** — The hidden word is 'daft'.
7) **carry our** — The hidden word is 'your'.
8) **fabric home** — The hidden word is 'rich'.
9) **gremlin evaporated** — The hidden word is 'line'.
10) **safe around** — The hidden word is 'fear'.
11) **koalas this** — The hidden word is 'last'.
12) **Caleb asked** — The hidden word is 'bask'.
13) **zoo makes** — The hidden word is 'zoom'.
14) **Heather enjoys** — The hidden word is 'here'.
15) **kept hugging** — The hidden word is 'thug'.
16) **phone on** — The hidden word is 'neon'.
17) **His shoelace** — The hidden word is 'hiss'.
18) **was eaten** — The hidden word is 'seat'.

Page 8 — Find The Missing Word

1) **TEN** — The complete word is BITTEN.
2) **NOW** — The complete word is SNOWBALL.
3) **RUM** — The complete word is TRUMPET.
4) **ROW** — The complete word is TOMORROW.
5) **ALL** — The complete word is BALLOON.
6) **RID** — The complete word is FRIDGE.
7) **RED** — The complete word is GLITTERED.
8) **ACT** — The complete word is TRACTOR.
9) **ANT** — The complete word is PLANTED.
10) **NET** — The complete word is PLANET.
11) **LOW** — The complete word is YELLOW.
12) **RAN** — The complete word is GRANDMA.
13) **HIS** — The complete word is WHISTLED.
14) **HAD** — The complete word is SHADOW.
15) **ROT** — The complete word is CARROTS.
16) **OIL** — The complete word is BOILED.
17) **DIE** — The complete word is MUDDIEST.
18) **HIM** — The complete word is CHIMED.

Page 9 — Use A Rule To Make A Word

1) **sag** — Take letters 1 and 2 from the first word, followed by letter 3 from the second word.
2) **elk** — Take letters 2 and 3 from the first word, followed by letter 1 from the second word.
3) **nor** — Take letter 1 from the second word, followed by letters 2 and 3 from the first word.
4) **can** — Take letters 2 and 3 from the second word, followed by letter 1 from the first word.
5) **map** — Take letter 3 from the first word, followed by letters 2 and 4 from the second word.
6) **bud** — Take letter 1 from the second word, followed by letters 2 and 1 from the first word.
7) **lad** — Take letter 4 from the second word, followed by letter 2 from the first word, and then letter 1 from the second word.
8) **den** — Take letters 3 and 2 from the first word, followed by letter 3 from the second word.
9) **tin** — Take letter 4 from the second word, followed by letters 3 and 4 from the first word.
10) **sad** — Take letters 3 and 2 from the first word, followed by letter 3 from the second word.
11) **lame** — Take letter 3 from the first word, followed by letters 2, 3 and 4 from the first word.
12) **ape** — Take letter 2 from the first word, followed by letter 2 from the second word, then letter 4 from the first word.
13) **gig** — Take letters 4 and 2 from the first word, followed by letter 2 from the second word.
14) **met** — Take letters 3 and 4 from the first word, followed by letter 1 from the second word.
15) **lot** — Take letters 3, 2 and 1 from the second word.
16) **big** — Take letters 4 and 2 from the first word, followed by letter 3 from the first word.
17) **lid** — Take letter 4 from the first word, followed by letter 3 from the second word, then letter 1 from the first word.
18) **rope** — Take letter 3 from the first word, followed by letter 2 from the second word, then letter 1 from the first word, then letter 4 from the second word.

Page 10 — Compound Words

1) **bathroom** — 'bathroom' is the only correctly spelled word that can be made.
2) **leapfrog** — 'leapfrog' is the only correctly spelled word that can be made.
3) **scarecrow** — 'scarecrow' is the only correctly spelled word that can be made.
4) **ladybird** — 'ladybird' is the only correctly spelled word that can be made.
5) **hopscotch** — 'hopscotch' is the only correctly spelled word that can be made.
6) **teardrop** — 'teardrop' is the only correctly spelled word that can be made.
7) **railway** — 'railway' is the only correctly spelled word that can be made.
8) **blackberry** — 'blackberry' is the only correctly spelled word that can be made.
9) **underline** — 'underline' is the only correctly spelled word that can be made.
10) **horseshoe** — 'horseshoe' is the only correctly spelled word that can be made.
11) **wheelchair** — 'wheelchair' is the only correctly spelled word that can be made.
12) **outdoor** — 'outdoor' is the only correctly spelled word that can be made.
13) **doorbell** — 'doorbell' is the only correctly spelled word that can be made.
14) **blackbird** — 'blackbird' is the only correctly spelled word that can be made.
15) **earthquake** — 'earthquake' is the only correctly spelled word that can be made.

16) **mankind** — 'mankind' is the only correctly spelled word that can be made.
17) **farmyard** — 'farmyard' is the only correctly spelled word that can be made.
18) **humbug** — 'humbug' is the only correctly spelled word that can be made.

Page 11 — Forming New Words

1) **tea** — The new words are 'teapot', 'teacake' and 'teaspoon'.
2) **rain** — The new words are 'rainfall', 'rainbow' and 'raincoat'.
3) **after** — The new words are 'afternoon', 'aftershave' and 'aftertaste'.
4) **snow** — The new words are 'snowflake', 'snowball' and 'snowman'.
5) **sand** — The new words are 'sandcastle', 'sandstorm' and 'sandbox'.
6) **sea** — The new words are 'seashore', 'seashell' and 'seaweed'.
7) **air** — The new words are 'airport', 'aircraft' and 'airbag'.
8) **black** — The new words are 'blackberry', 'blackbird' and 'blackmail'.
9) **berry** — The new words are 'blueberry', 'raspberry' and 'strawberry'.
10) **day** — The new words are 'birthday', 'weekday' and 'today'.
11) **time** — The new words are 'playtime', 'bedtime' and 'daytime'.
12) **house** — The new words are 'farmhouse', 'greenhouse' and 'lighthouse'.
13) **ball** — The new words are 'basketball', 'netball' and 'eyeball'.
14) **light** — The new words are 'daylight', 'streetlight' and 'moonlight'.
15) **bird** — The new words are 'hummingbird', 'bluebird' and 'songbird'.
16) **box** — The new words are 'jukebox', 'matchbox' and 'toolbox'.

Page 12 — Complete A Word Pair

1) **sail** — Remove letters 1 and 2, leaving the remaining letters in the order 3, 4, 5, 6.
2) **peat** — Remove letters 1 and 2, leaving the remaining letters in the order 3, 4, 5, 6.
3) **show** — Remove letters 5 and 6, leaving the remaining letters in the order 1, 2, 3, 4.
4) **over** — Remove letters 1 and 6, leaving the remaining letters in the order 2, 3, 4, 5.
5) **tool** — Rearrange letters 1, 2, 3, 4 in the order 4, 3, 2, 1.
6) **lad** — Remove letters 1, 2 and 6, leaving the remaining letters in the order 3, 4, 5.
7) **loop** — Rearrange letters 2, 3, 4, 5 in the order 5, 2, 3, 4.
8) **lend** — Replace the letter 'a' with the letter 'e'.
9) **nip** — Rearrange letters 1, 2, 6 in the order 6, 2, 1.
10) **rat** — Rearrange letters 1, 2, 6 in the order 6, 2, 1.
11) **bed** — Rearrange letters 1, 3, 5 in the order 1, 5, 3.
12) **let** — Rearrange letters 2, 3, 6 in the order 6, 2, 3.
13) **lamp** — Rearrange letters 2, 3, 4, 5 in the order 5, 2, 3, 4.
14) **fame** — The first letter of the word moves back one space along the alphabet.
15) **gem** — Rearrange letters 1, 4, 5 in the order 4, 5, 1.
16) **etch** — Rearrange letters 1, 2, 5, 6 in the order 5, 6, 1, 2.
17) **dig** — Rearrange letters 1, 3, 5 in the order 5, 3, 1.
18) **lost** — The last letter of the word moves forward one place along the alphabet.

Page 13 — Anagram In A Sentence

1) **SWORD** — SWORD is the only correctly spelled word that fits the sentence.
2) **MAGGOT** — MAGGOT is the only correctly spelled word that fits the sentence.
3) **MONKS** — MONKS is the only correctly spelled word that fits the sentence.
4) **GROWN** — GROWN is the only correctly spelled word that fits the sentence.
5) **SCRUB** — SCRUB is the only correctly spelled word that fits the sentence.
6) **WARMED** — WARMED is the only correctly spelled word that fits the sentence.
7) **VELVET** — VELVET is the only correctly spelled word that fits the sentence.
8) **TRAVEL** — TRAVEL is the only correctly spelled word that fits the sentence.
9) **FEWEST** — FEWEST is the only correctly spelled word that fits the sentence.
10) **NODDED** — NODDED is the only correctly spelled word that fits the sentence.
11) **PAUSED** — PAUSED is the only correctly spelled word that fits the sentence.
12) **HOTTER** — HOTTER is the only correctly spelled word that fits the sentence.
13) **SPROUTS** — SPROUTS is the only correctly spelled word that fits the sentence.
14) **GIRAFFE** — GIRAFFE is the only correctly spelled word that fits the sentence.
15) **BEDROOM** — BEDROOM is the only correctly spelled word that fits the sentence.
16) **CHARMER** — CHARMER is the only correctly spelled word that fits the sentence.
17) **DIAMOND** — DIAMOND is the only correctly spelled word that fits the sentence.
18) **CUNNING** — CUNNING is the only correctly spelled word that fits the sentence.

Page 14 — Words That Can't Be Made

1) **sit** — 'sit' can't be made because there is no 't' in 'easily'.
2) **ate** — 'ate' can't be made because there is no 'a' in 'compute'.
3) **bat** — 'bat' can't be made because there is no 'a' in 'buckets'.
4) **lad** — 'lad' can't be made because there is no 'l' in 'armband'.
5) **tick** — 'tick' can't be made because there is no 'i' in 'rockets'.
6) **dole** — 'dole' can't be made because there is no 'e' in 'dolphin'.
7) **role** — 'role' can't be made because there is no 'l' in 'toaster'.

8) **gags** — 'gags' can't be made because there is only one 'g' in 'hogwash'.
9) **rate** — 'rate' can't be made because there is no 'a' in 'trickier'.
10) **barb** — 'barb' can't be made because there is only one 'b' in 'breathes'.
11) **meat** — 'meat' can't be made because there is no 't' in 'chambers'.
12) **rare** — 'rare' can't be made because there is only one 'r' in 'gangster'.
13) **mats** — 'mats' can't be made because there is no 's' in 'nightmare'.
14) **cores** — 'cores' can't be made because there is no 'o' in 'captures'.
15) **each** — 'each' can't be made because there is no 'h' in 'carbuncle'.
16) **sheds** — 'sheds' can't be made because there is only one 's' in 'headphones'.
17) **walls** — 'walls' can't be made because there is only one 'l' in 'lawnmowers'.
18) **later** — 'later' can't be made because there is no 'r' in 'pollinates'.

Page 15 — Word Ladders

1) **(WIDE) (WINE)** — The ladder is: HIDE (WIDE) (WINE) WINK.
2) **(MILE) (MIME)** — The ladder is: MALE (MILE) (MIME) LIME.
3) **(FALL) (FELL)** — The ladder is: FAIL (FALL) (FELL) YELL.
4) **(LOOT) (SOOT)** — The ladder is: LOOM (LOOT) (SOOT) SORT.
5) **(SALT) (SALE)** — The ladder is: SILT (SALT) (SALE) PALE.
6) **(CLAP) (CLAY)** — The ladder is: CLIP (CLAP) (CLAY) PLAY.
7) **(HELD) (HOLD)** — The ladder is: HEAD (HELD) (HOLD) HOLE.
8) **(BOLT) (BELT)** — The ladder is: JOLT (BOLT) (BELT) BELL.
9) **(RENT) (RANT)** — The ladder is: TENT (RENT) (RANT) RANK.
10) **(POKE) (POSE)** — The ladder is: JOKE (POKE) (POSE) POST.
11) **(COST) (CAST)** — The ladder is: COAT (COST) (CAST) FAST.
12) **(MOLE) (MORE)** — The ladder is: MULE (MOLE) (MORE) WORE.
13) **(FLOG) (FROG)** — The ladder is: CLOG (FLOG) (FROG) FROM.
14) **(HARD) (LARD)** — The ladder is: HARP (HARD) (LARD) LORD.
15) **(SPUN) (STUN)** — The ladder is: SPIN (SPUN) (STUN) STUB.
16) **(STAB) (SLAB)** — The ladder is: STAR (STAB) (SLAB) FLAB.
17) **(DOVE) (MOVE)** — The ladder is: DIVE (DOVE) (MOVE) MODE.
18) **(SLAM) (SLAP)** — The ladder is: SLUM (SLAM) (SLAP) FLAP.

Page 16 — Closest Meaning

1) **angry   cross** — Both of these mean 'resentful or annoyed'.
2) **kind   nice** — Both of these mean 'pleasant'.
3) **buy   purchase** — Both of these mean 'to acquire using money'.
4) **ugly   foul** — Both of these mean 'unattractive'.
5) **allow   permit** — Both of these mean 'to give permission'.
6) **whisper   murmur** — Both of these mean 'to speak quietly'.
7) **funny   amusing** — Both of these mean 'comical'.
8) **litter   garbage** — Both of these mean 'rubbish or refuse'.
9) **precious   valuable** — Both of these mean 'of high value'.
10) **honest   truthful** — Both of these mean 'sincere'.
11) **rain   drizzle** — Both of these are types of wet weather.
12) **same   identical** — Both of these mean 'exactly alike'.
13) **wish   hope** — Both of these mean 'to desire'.
14) **graph   chart** — Both of these are ways of presenting data visually.
15) **cunning   sly** — Both of these mean 'crafty'.
16) **friendly   amiable** — Both of these mean 'warm and likeable'.
17) **tidy   neat** — Both of these mean 'ordered'.
18) **forgive   pardon** — Both of these mean 'to excuse someone's wrongdoing'.

Page 17 — Opposite Meaning

1) **upstairs   downstairs** — 'upstairs' means 'above', whereas 'downstairs' means 'below'.
2) **clean   filthy** — 'clean' means 'not dirty', whereas 'filthy' means 'dirty'.
3) **young   old** — 'young' means 'youthful', whereas 'old' means 'elderly'.
4) **beautiful   hideous** — 'beautiful' means 'attractive', whereas 'hideous' means 'unattractive'.
5) **full   empty** — 'full' means 'at capacity', whereas 'empty' means 'having no content'.
6) **wide   narrow** — 'wide' means 'broad', whereas 'narrow' means 'thin'.
7) **love   loathe** — 'love' means 'adore', whereas 'loathe' means 'hate'.
8) **deep   shallow** — 'deep' means 'extending a long way down', whereas 'shallow' means 'lacking depth'.
9) **shiny   dull** — 'shiny' means 'bright and gleaming', whereas 'dull' means 'matt or grimy'.
10) **stretch   squash** — 'stretch' means 'to pull apart', whereas 'squash' means 'to push together'.
11) **wealthy   poor** — 'wealthy' means 'having lots of money', whereas 'poor' means 'lacking money'.
12) **sell   buy** — 'sell' means 'to give goods in exchange for money', whereas 'buy' means 'to give money in exchange for goods'.
13) **minor   major** — 'minor' means 'less important', whereas 'major' means 'more important'.
14) **cheap   costly** — 'cheap' means 'inexpensive', whereas 'costly' means 'expensive'.
15) **enemy   friend** — 'enemy' means 'someone who is disliked', whereas 'friend' means 'someone who is known and liked'.

Answers

16) **busy   quiet** — 'busy' means 'crowded', whereas 'quiet' means 'free from crowds'.
17) **taut   slack** — 'taut' means 'tight', whereas 'slack' means 'loose'.
18) **bumpy   flat** — 'bumpy' means 'uneven', whereas 'flat' means 'even'.

Page 18 — Multiple Meanings

1) **sweet** — 'sweet' can mean 'flavoured with sugar' or 'good-natured'.
2) **play** — 'play' can mean 'a performance' or 'to be merry or lively'.
3) **tight** — 'tight' can mean 'not much room' or 'reluctant to spend money'.
4) **top** — 'top' can mean 'the highest point' or 'a cover for a jar, can etc'.
5) **upset** — 'upset' can mean 'to tip over' or 'to make unhappy'.
6) **cold** — 'cold' can mean 'lacking heat' or 'unaffectionate'.
7) **simple** — 'simple' can mean 'sparse and unadorned' or 'not difficult'.
8) **present** — 'present' can mean 'at this time' or 'something given as a gesture of goodwill'.
9) **form** — 'form' can mean 'a group' or 'a set of questions'.
10) **kind** — 'kind' can mean 'gentle or pleasant' or 'a group of something'.
11) **match** — 'match' can mean 'a sporting competition' or 'an alliance of two people'.
12) **sign** — 'sign' can mean 'to write your name' or 'an information notice'.
13) **second** — 'second' can mean 'a short amount of time' or 'following the leader'.
14) **key** — 'key' can mean 'something that is essential' or 'an explanation of symbols or codes'.
15) **band** — 'band' can mean 'a group which plays instruments' or 'a ring-shaped object'.
16) **refuse** — 'refuse' can mean 'household waste' or 'to say no to something'.
17) **row** — 'row' can mean 'to argue' or 'to move using an oar'.
18) **sow** — 'sow' can mean 'a female pig' or 'to put in the ground for growing'.

Page 19 — Odd Ones Out

1) **numbers   figures** — The other three are examples of numbers.
2) **hot   warm** — The other three mean 'lacking heat'.
3) **hate   dislike** — The other three mean 'to feel positively about something'.
4) **whisper   mutter** — The other three all mean 'to speak loudly'.
5) **office   library** — The other three are all places where people live.
6) **desert   glacier** — The other three are places where trees grow.
7) **grass   oak** — The other three are types of flowers.
8) **fridge   tiles** — The other three are appliances used to heat food.
9) **football   cricket** — The other three are all things you would find in a playground.
10) **recorder   trumpet** — The other three are all stringed instruments.
11) **shorts   sandals** — The other three all are all items of clothes worn to keep warm.
12) **laugh   chuckle** — The other three all mean 'joyful'.
13) **gloves   earrings** — The other three are all things you wear on your feet.
14) **diced   peeled** — The other three are all ways of cooking.
15) **orchestra   song** — The other three are all types of pictures.
16) **fibreglass   plastic** — The other three are all natural materials.
17) **rehearse   practice** — The other three all mean 'to perform'.
18) **enter   come** — The other three all mean 'to depart'.

Page 20 — Word Connections

1) **floor   window** — They are the parts of a house covered by carpet and curtains.
2) **correct   incorrect** — They are synonyms of 'right' and 'wrong'.
3) **tennis   badminton** — They are the sports which use balls and shuttlecocks.
4) **drink   eat** — They are the actions associated with 'water' and 'food'.
5) **loud   quiet** — They are the volumes associated with shouting and whispering.
6) **tired   sad** — They are the feelings associated with yawning and crying.
7) **difficult   straightforward** — They are synonyms of 'hard' and 'easy'.
8) **book   internet** — They are where pages and websites are found.
9) **cat   sheep** — They are animals that have coats of fur and wool.
10) **here   away** — They are synonyms of 'present' and 'absent'.
11) **spider   pig** — They are animals that have eight and four legs.
12) **big   small** — They are the sizes of cities and villages.
13) **petal   leaf** — They are parts of flowers and trees.
14) **prince   princess** — They are the uncrowned versions of kings and queens.
15) **snow   sun** — They are weather traditionally associated with winter and summer.
16) **book   film** — They are entertainment forms associated with reading and watching.
17) **hop   fly** — They are the ways in which frogs and sparrows move.
18) **gold   bronze** — They are the metals from which the medals received for first and third place are made.

Page 21 — Reorder Words To Make A Sentence

1) **Season Winter** — The sentence is: 'Winter is my favourite season'.
2) **school rode** — The sentence is: 'I rode to school on a rhino'.
3) **Book read** — The sentence is: 'Read this book for your homework tonight'.
4) **road cross** — The sentence is: 'Look both ways when you cross the road'.
5) **subjects Science** — The sentence is: 'Maths and Science are my favourite subjects'.
6) **wooden cat** — The sentence is: 'The cat darted under the wooden table'.
7) **France camping** — The sentence is: 'We went camping in France last summer'.
8) **shoes socks** — The sentence is 'Put on your socks before your shoes'.
9) **blue French** — The sentence is: 'The French flag is blue, white and red'.
10) **red munched** — The sentence is: 'The ogre munched on a red apple'.
11) **Africa mongooses** — The sentence is: 'Mongooses come from Africa'.
12) **whistle referee** — The sentence is: 'The referee blew his whistle at full-time'.
13) **station make** — The sentence is: 'We won't make it to the station on time'.
14) **night tomorrow** — The sentence is: 'The circus opens tomorrow night'.
15) **canal down** — The sentence is: 'The barge sailed gracefully down the canal'.
16) **early got** — The sentence is: 'Gemma got up early to go toe-wrestling'.
17) **Bus tomorrow** — The sentence is: 'Tomorrow I'm taking the bus to school'.
18) **bag carried** — The sentence is: 'The postman carried his bag of letters'.

Page 22 — Complete The Sum

1) **4** — $20 \div 5 = 4$
2) **2** — $22 \div 11 = 2$
3) **25** — $5 \times 5 = 25$
4) **21** — $8 + 13 = 21$
5) **4** — $10 \times 2 = 20$, $20 = 24 - 4$
6) **1** — $15 \div 3 = 5$, $5 = 4 + 1$
7) **5** — $7 \times 3 = 21$, $21 = 16 + 5$
8) **7** — $26 \div 2 = 13$, $13 = 20 - 7$
9) **2** — $24 \div 3 = 8$, $8 = 4 \times 2$
10) **3** — $18 \div 6 = 3$, $3 = 9 \div 3$
11) **17** — $7 \times 3 - 4 = 17$
12) **4** — $10 \div 5 + 2 = 4$
13) **15** — $6 \times 3 - 3 = 15$
14) **7** — $8 \times 4 = 32$, $32 = 5 \times 5 + 7$
15) **10** — $24 \div 3 \times 5 = 40$, $40 = 4 \times 10$
16) **12** — $15 \times 2 \div 5 = 6$, $6 = 12 - 6$
17) **2** — $12 \div 4 = 3$, $3 = 20 \div 4 - 2$
18) **8** — $25 \div 5 + 4 = 9$, $9 = 17 - 8$

Page 23 — Letter Sequences

1) **EU** — Each letter in the pair repeats once then moves forward 1 letter.
2) **SA** — The first letter moves forward 1 letter each time. The second letter moves back 1 letter each time.
3) **RY** — Each letter in the pair moves forward 3 letters each time.
4) **LB** — The first letter in the pair moves forward 1 letter each time. The second letter moves forward 2 letters each time.
5) **ZO** — Each letter in the pair moves forward 2 letters each time.
6) **IP** — The first letter in the pair moves back 4 letters each time. The second letter moves forward 4 letters each time.
7) **LD** — The first letter in the pair moves forward 2 letters each time. The second letter moves back 3 letters each time.
8) **SU** — The first letter in the pair moves back 2 letters each time. The second letter moves forward 4 letters each time.
9) **AV** — The first letter in the pair moves forward 3 letters each time. The second letter moves forward 2 letters each time.
10) **KD** — The first letter in the pair moves back 2 letters each time. The second letter moves back 3 letters each time.
11) **KO** — The first letter in the pair moves back 3 letters each time. The second letter moves back 3 letters then forward 1 letter alternately.
12) **JM** — The first letter in the pair moves forward 1 letter then forward 2 letters. The second letter moves forward 2 letters each time.
13) **SC** — The first letter in the pair moves forward 1 letter then 5 letters alternately. The second letter moves back 5 letters then 1 letter alternately.
14) **WX** — The first letter in the pair moves forward 2 letters then 3 letters alternately. The second letter moves back 2 letters then 3 letters alternately.
15) **NW** — The first letter in the pair moves back 2 letters then 1 letter alternately. The second letter moves forward 3 letters then 2 letters alternately.
16) **PF** — The first letter in the pair moves forward 1 additional letter each time, i.e. +1, +2, +3. The second letter moves back 4 letters each time.
17) **QT** — The first letter in the pair moves forward 2 letters then 3 letters alternately. The second letter moves back 3 letters then 2 letters alternately.
18) **JP** — The first letter in the pair moves in the sequence −5, −4, −3, −2, −1. The second letter moves forward 1 additional letter each time, i.e. 0, +1, +2, +3, +4.

Page 24 — Number Sequences

1) **30** — Add 5 each time.
2) **32** — The number doubles each time.
3) **10** — Subtract 10 each time.
4) **42** — Add 7 each time.
5) **23** — Add the two previous numbers together, i.e. $1 + 4 = 5$, $4 + 5 = 9$ etc.
6) **20** — +4, 0, +4, 0, +4
7) **32** — Add the two previous numbers together, i.e. $4 + 4 = 8$, $4 + 8 = 12$ etc.
8) **27** — Add numbers in ascending order: +1, +2, +3, +4, +5.
9) **3** — The number is halved each time.

10) **32** — Add even numbers in ascending order:
  +2, +4, +6, +8, +10.

11) **4** — There are two sequences which alternate. In the first, the number increases by 1 each time. In the second, the number increases by 5 each time.

12) **14** — −1, 0, +1, +2, +3.

13) **3** — There are two sequences which alternate. In the first, the number decreases by 3 each time. In the second, the number increases by 4 each time.

14) **27** — Add odd numbers in ascending order:
  +1, +3, +5, +7, +9.

15) **6** — Subtract numbers in descending order:
  −9, −8, −7, −6, −5.

16) **48** — Multiply by ascending numbers, i.e. ×1, ×2, ×3, ×4.

17) **8** — There are two sequences which alternate. In the first, the number increases by 2 each time. In the second, the number increases by 3 each time.

18) **5** — Subtract odd numbers in descending order:
  −13, −11, −9, −7, −5.

Page 25 — Related Numbers

1) **8** — Add the two outside numbers.
2) **8** — Subtract the third number from the first number.
3) **5** — Subtract the first number from the third number.
4) **13** — Find the middle point between the two outer numbers, by adding the outer numbers together and dividing by 2.
5) **24** — Add the two outside numbers.
6) **28** — Find the middle point between the two outer numbers, by adding the outer numbers together and dividing by 2.
7) **12** — Multiply the two outer numbers.
8) **9** — Subtract the first number from the third number.
9) **3** — Divide the third number by the first number.
10) **18** — Find the middle point between the two outer numbers, by adding the outer numbers together and dividing by 2.
11) **12** — Multiply the two outer numbers.
12) **3** — Divide the first number by the third number.
13) **32** — Find the middle point between the two outer numbers, by adding the outer numbers together and dividing by 2.
14) **9** — Multiply the outer numbers.
15) **5** — Divide the first number by the third number. Add 1.
16) **10** — Add the two outer numbers together. Double the answer.
17) **6** — Subtract the third number from the first number. Halve the answer.
18) **16** — Subtract the third number from the first number. Double the answer.

Page 26 — Letter-Coded Sums

1) **E** — 7 + 3 = 10, E = 10
2) **C** — 12 ÷ 2 = 6, C = 6
3) **B** — 17 − 14 = 3, B = 3
4) **D** — 5 × 3 = 15, D = 15
5) **B** — 16 ÷ 2 = 8, B = 8
6) **D** — 19 − 7 + 2 = 14, D = 14
7) **E** — 3 + 8 + 9 = 20, E = 20
8) **A** — 24 ÷ 3 − 6 = 2, A = 2
9) **E** — 2 × 5 + 6 = 16, E = 16
10) **E** — 16 × 2 − 8 = 24, E = 24
11) **D** — 4 × 6 − 13 = 11, D = 11
12) **A** — 6 × 7 ÷ 21 = 2, A = 2
13) **C** — 2 × 9 − 7 − 4 = 7, C = 7
14) **E** — 3 ÷ 1 × 4 + 1 = 13, E = 13
15) **A** — 2 × 3 + 12 − 16 = 2, A = 2

Page 27 — Letter-Word Codes

1) **UBOL** — To get from the word to the code move each letter forward 1.
2) **ATRG** — To get from the word to the code move each letter back 1.
3) **SLUG** — To get from the code to the word move each letter forward 2.
4) **PRRQ** — To get from the word to the code move each letter forward 3.
5) **BLUE** — To get from the code to the word move each letter back 4.
6) **ATZUR** — To get from the word to the code move the letters in the sequence −1, +2, −1, +2, −1.
7) **JHRUO** — To get from the word to the code move the letters in the sequence +3, 0, +3, 0, +3.
8) **SQUAT** — To get from the code to the word move the letters in the sequence −2, +2, −2, +2, −2.
9) **BAD** — This is a mirror code, where the letters are an equal distance from the centre of the alphabet. B is a mirror of Y, A is a mirror of Z and D is a mirror of W.
10) **EUGDO** — To get from the word to the code move the letters in the sequence +2, +3, +2, +3, +2.
11) **CARD** — This is a mirror code, where the letters are an equal distance from the centre of the alphabet. C is a mirror of X, A is a mirror of Z, R is a mirror of I and D is a mirror of W.
12) **MARKS** — To get from the code to the word move the letters in the sequence 0, +1, +2, +3, +4.
13) **UCDYM** — To get from the word to the code move the letters in the sequence +1, −2, +3, −4, +5.
14) **DRAW** — This is a mirror code, where the letters are an equal distance from the centre of the alphabet. D is a mirror of W, R is a mirror of I, A is a mirror of Z and W is a mirror of D.

Pages 28 & 29 — Number-Word Codes

1) **1264** — B = 1, I = 2, N = 6, D = 4
2) **4351** — D = 4, R = 3, A = 5, B = 1
3) **BRAN** — B = 1, R = 3, A = 5, N = 6
4) **2346** — T = 2, E = 3, A = 4, R = 6
5) **2163** — T = 2, O = 1, R = 6, E = 3
6) **RAFT** — R = 6, A = 4, F = 5, T = 2
7) **3264** — S = 3, O = 2, A = 6, K = 4
8) **3615** — S = 3, A = 6, M = 1, E = 5
9) **MASK** — M = 1, A = 6, S = 3, K = 4
10) **6231** — R = 6, A = 2, C = 3, E = 1
11) **2351** — A = 2, C = 3, H = 5, E = 1
12) **CARE** — C = 3, A = 2, R = 6, E = 1
13) **1645** — L = 1, A = 6, K = 4, E = 5
14) **3645** — C = 3, A = 6, K = 4, E = 5
15) **KEEL** — K = 4, E = 5, E = 5, L = 1
16) **3564** — A = 3, N = 5, E = 6, W = 4
17) **2635** — M = 2, E = 6, A = 3, N = 5
18) **WANE** — W = 4, A = 3, N = 5, E = 6
19) **3654** — O = 3, M = 6, E = 5, N = 4
20) **4165** — N = 4, A = 1, M = 6, E = 5
21) **NEON** — N = 4, E = 5, O = 3, N = 4
22) **3154** — L = 3, A = 1, T = 5, E = 4
23) **5133** — T = 5, A = 1, L = 3, L = 3
24) **FLAT** — F = 6, L = 3, A = 1, T = 5

Pages 30 & 31 — Explore The Facts

1) **Lisa** — Lisa goes riding three times a week: on Saturday, Sunday and Wednesday.
2) **William** — William is only going on one holiday: cycling with Mark.
3) **Haj** — Haj likes three toppings: raisins, lemon curd and sausages.
4) **Edward** — Edward only has two activities planned: swimming and shopping.
5) **Neal** — Neal is only going to visit one place: an art gallery.
6) **Spencer** — Spencer came top in two subjects: Science and History.
7) **Julia** — Julia only swims once a week: on Wednesday.
8) **Maddie** — Maddie has three pets: a dog, a pony and a cat.

Pages 32 & 33 — Solve The Riddle

1) **E** — Max runs faster than Charlotte and Ahmed is slower than Charlotte, so Max must run faster than Ahmed.
2) **C** — Josh's house has half as many bedrooms as Karl's house, so Karl's house can't have 5 bedrooms because Josh's can't have 2.5 rooms.
3) **E** — Jamie was born before Georgia, Laura and Rohan, so he's the oldest.
4) **D** — July was 7 degrees hotter than June, and August was 2 degrees hotter than June, so July can't have been cooler than August.
5) **B** — Patrick's bus arrived at 7.15, Hannah's bus arrived 10 minutes later at 7.25, and Jacob's bus arrived 15 minutes after Hannah's, so Jacob's bus arrived at 7.40.
6) **D** — Lucy buys four banners for £3 each, so she spends a total of £12. Lily spends half as much as Lucy, so she spends £6. Grace and Dan spend £20 between them, and Dan spends £6.50, so Grace must spend £13.50, which is £7.50 more than Lily.

Page 34 — Letter Connections

1) **NP** — Each letter in the pair moves forward 2 letters.
2) **HJ** — Each letter in the pair moves forward 2 letters.
3) **NQ** — Each letter in the pair moves back 1 letter.
4) **PW** — Each letter in the pair moves forward 4 letters.
5) **DW** — This is a mirror pair, where the letters are an equal distance from the centre of the alphabet. C is 2 letters forward from A, so the answer is DW, because D is 2 letters forward from B, and W is its mirror pair.
6) **SR** — Each letter in the pair moves forward 5 letters.
7) **OS** — The first letter in the pair moves back 1 letter, the second letter moves forward 1 letter.
8) **NH** — Each letter in the pair moves forward 2 letters.
9) **SV** — The first letter in the pair moves forward 2 letters, the second letter moves back 3 letters.
10) **ZA** — This is a mirror pair, where the letters are an equal distance from the centre of the alphabet. V is 3 letters forward from S, so the answer is ZA, because Z is 3 letters forward from W, and A is its mirror pair.
11) **XF** — The first letter in the pair moves back 4 letters, the second letter moves back 1 letter.
12) **OL** — This is a mirror pair, where the letters are an equal distance from the centre of the alphabet. I is 3 letters back from L, so the answer is OL, because O is 3 letters back from R, and L is its mirror pair.
13) **YV** — Each letter in the pair moves back 5 letters.
14) **UY** — The first letter in the pair moves forward 3 letters, the second letter moves back 3 letters.
15) **QJ** — This is a mirror pair, where the letters are an equal distance from the centre of the alphabet. M is 4 letters back from Q, so the answer is QJ, because Q is 4 letters back from U, and J is its mirror pair.
16) **IS** — The first letter in the pair moves forward 3 letters, the second letter moves forward 1 letter.
17) **IZ** — The first letter in the pair moves back 3 letters, the second letter moves forward 2 letters.
18) **AZ** — This is a mirror pair, where the letters are an equal distance from the centre of the alphabet. Y is 5 letters forward from T, so the answer is AZ, because A is 5 letters forward from V, and Z is its mirror pair.

Pages 35 — Word Grids

1)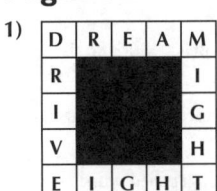
2)

This is the only way all the words fit together in the grid.

3)
4)

This is the only way all the words fit together in the grid.

5)
6)

This is the only way all the words fit together in the grid.

7)
8)

This is the only way all the words fit together in the grid.

9)

This is the only way all the words fit together in the grid.

Pages 36-40 — Assessment Test 1

1) **E** — 3 × 8 = 24, E = 24
2) **A** — 14 ÷ 7 = 2, A = 2
3) **A** — 24 − 18 = 6, A = 6
4) **C** — 22 ÷ 2 + 6 = 17, C = 17
5) **B** — 18 ÷ 3 − 3 = 3, B = 3
6) **4536** — T = 4, O = 5, Y = 3, S = 6
7) **6412** — S = 6, T = 4, A = 1, G = 2
8) **GOAT** — G = 2, O = 5, A = 1, T = 4
9) **2534** — P = 2, A = 5, I = 3, R = 4
10) **2431** — P = 2, R = 4, I = 3, M = 1
11) **PAIN** — P = 2, A = 5, I = 3, N = 6
12) **Josh edited** — The hidden word is 'shed'.
13) **with emus** — The hidden word is 'them'.
14) **cow entered** — The hidden word is 'went'.
15) **for tea** — The hidden word is 'fort'.
16) **is hot** — The hidden word is 'shot'.
17) **28** — +7, 0, +7, 0, +7
18) **6** — Subtract 6 each time.
19) **80** — The number doubles each time.
20) **25** — Subtract 5 each time.
21) **19** — Add numbers in ascending order: +1, +2, +3, +4, +5.
22) **big   large** — Both of these mean 'above average size'.
23) **wet   damp** — Both of these mean 'moist'.
24) **small   little** — Both of these mean 'below average size'.
25) **happy   glad** — Both of these mean 'joyful'.
26) **run   sprint** — Both of these mean 'to move fast on foot'.
27) **sketch   draw** — Both of these mean 'to depict something, usually in pencil'.
28) **C** — Tom walks to school every day except Friday, so he can't get the bus on Tuesday.
29) **D** — Rosie goes to bed before Katya, Katya goes to bed before Oliver, and Oliver goes at the same time as Amaya. This means that Amaya must go to bed after Rosie.
30) **LS** — Each letter in the pair moves back 1.
31) **HS** — This is a mirror pair, where the letters are an equal distance from the centre of the alphabet. E is 1 letter forward from D, so the answer is HS, because H is 1 letter forward from G, and S is its mirror pair.
32) **RU** — Each letter in the pair moves forward 4.
33) **NR** — The first letter stays the same, the second letter moves forward 2.
34) **GT** — This is a mirror pair, where the letters are an equal distance from the centre of the alphabet. J is 3 letters back from M, so the answer is GT, because G is 3 letters back from J, and T is its mirror pair.
35) **head   hand** — They are the parts of the body on which hats and gloves are worn.
36) **drive   ride** — They are the actions associated with using a car and a bike.
37) **blue   green** — They are the colour of the sky and grass.
38) **hospital   school** — They are the places where doctors and teachers work.
39) **elephant   ant** — They are animals that have trunks and antennae.
40) **top** — Take letter 3 from the first word, followed by letters 2 and 3 from the second word.
41) **tag** — Take letters 4 and 2 from the first word, followed by letter 1 from the second word.
42) **ace** — Take letters 3 and 2 from the second word, followed by letter 4 from the first word.
43) **ram** — Take letters 3 and 2 from the first word, followed by letter 3 from the second word.
44) **fat** — Take letter 1 from the second word, followed by letter 2 from the first word, and then letter 3 from the second word.
45) **tab** — Take letter 3 from the first word, followed by letter 2 from the second word, and then letter 1 from the first word.
46) **6** — Add the two outer numbers together.
47) **16** — Add the two outer numbers together.
48) **12** — Subtract the first number from the third.
49) **7** — Find the middle point between the two outer numbers, by adding the outer numbers together and dividing by 2.
50) **32** — Multiply the two outer numbers together.
51) **set** — 'set' can mean 'to become solid' or 'a class or group'.

Answers

52) **hard** — 'hard' can mean 'physically tough' or 'difficult to do'.
53) **spot** — 'spot' can mean 'to notice something' or 'a blemish on the skin'.
54) **can** — 'can' can mean 'a container for food or drink' or 'to be able to do something'.
55) **bat** — 'bat' can mean 'a stick for playing sports' or 'to hit something'.
56) **h** — The new words are 'bath', 'hat', 'ash' and 'ham'.
57) **m** — The new words are 'jam', 'most', 'harm' and 'make'.
58) **p** — The new words are 'stop', 'pod', 'leap' and 'pit'.
59) **a** — The new words are 'rota', 'and', 'sea' and 'ape'.
60) **r** — The new words are 'stir', 'rail', 'oar' and 'rat'.

Pages 41-45 — Assessment Test 2

1) **Daneesh** — Daneesh likes cereal, yoghurt and toast.
2) **Max** — Max buys sweets, football magazines and presents with his pocket money.
3) **TE** — The first letter moves forward 2 letters each time. The second letter moves forward 1 letter each time.
4) **CF** — Each letter in the pair moves back 5 letters each time.
5) **FU** — The first letter moves back 1 letter each time. The second letter moves forward 2 letters each time.
6) **HT** — The first letter moves back 3 letters each time. The second letter moves back 1 letter each time.
7) **LU** — The first letter moves back 2 letters each time. The second letter moves forward 2 letters each time.
8) **QL** — The first letter moves forward 4 letters each time. The second letter moves back 3 letters each time.
9) **mini tiny** — The other three all mean 'above average size'.
10) **fox badger** — The other three are all pets.
11) **finger foot** — The other three are all facial features.
12) **scarf jumper** — The other three are all items of jewellery.
13) **apple strawberry** — The other three are all vegetables.
14) **6** — $18 \div 3 = 6$
15) **13** — $21 - 8 = 13$
16) **14** — $7 \times 2 = 14$
17) **22** — $12 \times 2 - 2 = 22$
18) **16** — $8 \div 2 + 12 = 16$
19) **PAD** — The complete word is SPADES.
20) **WIN** — The complete word is WINTER.
21) **HOP** — The complete word is SHOPPING.
22) **AID** — The complete word is MERMAID.
23) **HOW** — The complete word is SHOWING.
24) **1534** — W = 1, H = 5, I = 3, P = 4
25) **1326** — W = 1, I = 3, R = 2, E = 6
26) **RIPE** — R = 2, I = 3, P = 4, E = 6
27) **3243** — T = 3, E = 2, S = 4, T = 3
28) **1643** — R = 1, U = 6, S = 4, T = 3
29) **OURS** — O = 5, U = 6, R = 1, S = 4
30) **sunshine** — 'sunshine' is the only correctly spelled word that can be made.
31) **birthday** — 'birthday' is the only correctly spelled word that can be made.
32) **airport** — 'airport' is the only correctly spelled word that can be made.
33) **eyebrow** — 'eyebrow' is the only correctly spelled word that can be made.
34) **butterfly** — 'butterfly' is the only correctly spelled word that can be made.
35) **clockwork** — 'clockwork' is the only correctly spelled word that can be made.
36) **ape** — Remove letters 1, 2 and 3, leaving the remaining letters in the order 4, 5, 6.
37) **came** — Remove letters 5 and 6, leaving the remaining letters in the order 1, 2, 3, 4.
38) **won** — Rearrange letters 3, 4 and 5 in the order 4, 3, 5.
39) **dip** — Rearrange letters 1, 3 and 6 in the order 6, 3, 1.
40) **how** — Remove letters 2, 3, 4 and 7, leaving the remaining letters in the order 1, 5, 6.
41) **sunrise sunset** — 'sunrise' is when the sun comes up, whereas 'sunset' is when the sun goes down.
42) **huge tiny** — 'huge' means 'very big', whereas 'tiny' means 'very small'.
43) **boy girl** — 'a boy' is a male child, whereas 'a girl' is a female child.
44) **evening morning** — 'evening' is the period at the end of the day, whereas 'morning' is the start of the day.
45) **summer winter** — 'summer' is the hot season of the year, whereas 'winter' is the cold season.
46) **r** — The new words are 'ride' and 'crash'.
47) **t** — The new words are 'rain' and 'cart'.
48) **s** — The new words are 'pant' and 'toys'.
49) **t** — The new words are 'rash' and 'turn'.
50) **l** — The new words are 'food' and 'late'.
51) **beach shore** — Both of these are zones at the edge of the sea.
52) **meal lunch** — Both of these refer to food eaten at one sitting.
53) **gem jewel** — Both of these are words for precious minerals.
54) **coat jacket** — Both of these are outer garments with sleeves, worn on the top half of the body.
55) **smile grin** — Both of these are facial expressions conveying pleasure.
56) **MH** — Each letter in the pair moves back 3 letters.
57) **KP** — This is a mirror pair, where the letters are an equal distance from the centre of the alphabet. M is 1 letter forward from L, so the answer is KP, because K is 1 letter forward from J, and P is its mirror pair.
58) **FU** — This is a mirror pair, where the letters are an equal distance from the centre of the alphabet. B is 2 letters back from D, so the answer is FU, because F is 2 letters back from H, and U is its mirror pair.
59) **PL** — The first letter moves back 4 letters, the second letter moves forward 2 letters.
60) **JR** — The first letter moves forward 2 letters, the second letter moves back 2 letters.

Answers

Pages 46-50 — Assessment Test 3

1) **change** — 'change' can mean 'to make different' or 'money in the form of coins'.
2) **rap** — 'rap' can mean 'a sharp knock' or 'a type of music'.
3) **fire** — 'fire' can mean 'to discharge someone from a job' or 'the burning of fuel'.
4) **watch** — 'watch' can mean 'to look at something' or 'a device for telling the time'.
5) **gift** — 'gift' can mean 'a talent' or 'a present'.
6) **E** — 5 × 4 ÷ 2 = 10, E = 10
7) **A** — 3 × 9 − 25 = 2, A = 2
8) **B** — 6 + 20 − 21 = 5, B = 5
9) **B** — 4 + 5 + 9 − 13 = 5, B = 5
10) **E** — 8 × 4 − 10 = 22, E = 22
11) **2542** — T = 2, E = 5, X = 4, T = 2
12) **6512** — N = 6, E = 5, A = 1, T = 2
13) **NEXT** — N = 6, E = 5, X = 4, T = 2
14) **2364** — D = 2, I = 3, N = 6, T = 4
15) **5341** — B = 5, I = 3, T = 4, E = 1
16) **BIND** — B = 5, I = 3, N = 6, D = 2
17) **FN** — The first letter in the pair moves back 1 letter each time. The second letter moves forward 1 letter each time.
18) **FY** — The first letter in the pair moves forward 3 letters then 1 letter alternately. The second letter moves back 2 letters each time.
19) **HX** — The first letter in the pair moves back 2 letters each time. The second letter moves forward 4 letters each time.
20) **EK** — The first letter in the pair moves back 3 letters each time. The second letter moves forward 3 letters then back 1 letter alternately.
21) **RT** — The first letter in the pair moves forward 2 letters each time. The second letter moves back 3 letters each time.
22) **INCUU** — To get from the word to the code, move each letter forward 2.
23) **DOG** — This is a mirror code, where the letters are an equal distance from the centre of the alphabet. D is a mirror of W, O is a mirror of L and G is a mirror of T.
24) **SHELL** — To get from the code to the word, move the letters in the sequence −1, +1, −1, +1, −1.
25) **OAK** — This is a mirror code, where the letters are an equal distance from the centre of the alphabet. O is a mirror of L, A is a mirror of Z and K is a mirror of P.
26) **LOOPY** — To get from the code to the word, move the letters in the sequence +5, −2, +5, −2, +5.
27) **SLIP** — To get from the code to the word, move the letters in the sequence 0, +3, 0, +3.
28) **m** — The new words are 'film', 'mill', 'glum' and 'moat'.
29) **y** — The new words are 'toy', 'year', 'say' and 'yes'.
30) **n** — The new words are 'tin', 'nail', 'fun' and 'new'.
31) **b** — The new words are 'jab', 'boy', 'sob' and 'bat'.
32) **t** — The new words are 'sit', 'ten', 'pet' and 'trap'.
33) **him** — Take letters 4 and 2 from the first word, followed by letter 1 from the second word.
34) **aim** — Take letter 3 from the second word, followed by letters 2 and 1 from the first word.
35) **got** — Take letter 1 from the second word, followed by letters 2 and 4 from the first word.
36) **tea** — Take letters 1 and 4 from the second word, followed by letter 2 from the first word.
37) **wad** — Take letter 1 from the first word, followed by letters 2 and 1 from the second word.
38) **14** — Subtract 7 each time.
39) **29** — Add the two previous numbers together, i.e. 3 + 4 = 7, 4 + 7 = 11 etc.
40) **47** — Add 8 each time.
41) **20** — +2, +4, +2, +4, +2
42) **1** — Divide by 2 each time.
43) **14** — There are two sequences which alternate. In the first sequence, add 4 each time. In the second, add 2 each time.
44) **E** — Theo's team has won 2 more matches than Callum's team, and Callum's team has won 5 matches, so Theo's team must have won 7 matches. Helga's team has won 4 matches, so they haven't won more matches than Theo's team.
45) **C** — Train D is faster than train A, and train A is faster than train C, so train C must be slower than train D.
46) **Who opened** — The hidden word is 'hoop'.
47) **her broccoli** — The hidden word is 'herb'.
48) **Alec rowed** — The hidden word is 'crow'.
49) **drinks cans** — The hidden word is 'scan'.
50) **Grandpa thinks** — The hidden word is 'path'.
51) **man woman** — They are what boys and girls grow into.
52) **cold hot** — They are the temperatures of ice and fire.
53) **timid assured** — They are synonyms of shy and confident.
54) **library supermarket** — They are where you get books and food from.
55) **herd flock** — They are the collective nouns for groups of cows and sheep.
56) **far near** — 'far' means 'at a great distance', whereas 'near' means 'close by'.
57) **go stop** — 'go' means 'to start', whereas 'stop' means 'to cease'.
58) **shout whisper** — 'shout' means 'to communicate loudly', whereas 'whisper' means 'to communicate quietly'.
59) **short lofty** — 'short' means 'below average height', whereas 'lofty' means 'above average height'.
60) **speak listen** — 'speak' means 'to talk', whereas 'listen' means 'to try to hear'.

Pages 51-55 — Assessment Test 4

1) **b** — The new words are 'rain' and 'bark'.
2) **d** — The new words are 'fare' and 'dare'.
3) **r** — The new words are 'fame' and 'rice'.
4) **n** — The new words are 'blow' and 'pant'.
5) **r** — The new words are 'cape' and 'port'.
6) **5** — 17 − 12 = 5, 5 = 10 − 5
7) **3** — 6 + 6 = 12, 12 = 4 × 3
8) **7** — 19 + 2 = 21, 21 = 3 × 7
9) **2** — 1 + 22 = 23, 23 = 25 − 2
10) **14** — 7 × 4 = 28, 28 = 2 × 14
11) **3264** — K = 3, A = 2, L = 6, E = 4
12) **3446** — K = 3, E = 4, E = 4, L = 6
13) **CAFE** — C = 5, A = 2, F = 1, E = 4

14) 5421 — T = 5, O = 4, S = 2, H = 1
15) 6352 — N = 6, I = 3, T = 5, S = 2
16) THIS — T = 5, H = 1, I = 3, S = 2
17) work think — The other three involve using your voice.
18) garden garage — The other three are all rooms in a house.
19) plate spoon — The other three are containers for drinking from.
20) badminton tennis — The other three are sports played without a racket.
21) steam air — The other three are types of weather.
22) man lady — The other three are all words for people who are not adults.
23) Carlos — Carlos only does one activity: horseriding.
24) Abdul — Abdul does three things on his phone: texting, calling friends and playing games.
25) sheepdog — 'sheepdog' is the only correctly spelled word that can be made.
26) popcorn — 'popcorn' is the only correctly spelled word that can be made.
27) photograph — 'photograph' is the only correctly spelled word that can be made.
28) grandfather — 'grandfather' is the only correctly spelled word that can be made.
29) staircase — 'staircase' is the only correctly spelled word that can be made.
30) 12 — Add the two outer numbers together.
31) 3 — Subtract the third number from the first.
32) 12 — Find the middle point between the two outer numbers by adding the two numbers together and dividing by 2.
33) 15 — Multiply the two outer numbers.
34) 9 — Find the middle point between the two outer numbers by adding the two numbers together and dividing by 2.
35) ONE — The complete word is TELEPHONE.
36) LAP — The complete word is CLAPPED.
37) INK — The complete word is DRINK.
38) ART — The complete word is PARTY.
39) ACE — The complete word is SPACE.
40) curious interested — Both words mean 'eager to learn more'.
41) tired drowsy — Both words mean 'in need of sleep'.
42) cup mug — Both are vessels that you drink from.
43) boring tedious — Both words mean 'uninteresting'.
44) chore task — Both words mean 'a routine duty'.
45) worry concern — Both words mean 'anxiety'.
46) 39 — Add 7 each time.
47) 64 — Double the number each time.
48) 8 — Subtract 9 each time.
49) 40 — There are two sequences which alternate. In the first sequence, add 10 each time. In the second, add 12 each time.
50) 46 — Add even numbers in ascending order: +2, +4, +6, +8, +10.
51) NFLQ — To get from the word to the code, move the letters in the sequence −2, −3, −2, −3.
52) HEAD — This is a mirror code, where the letters are an equal distance from the centre of the alphabet. H is the mirror of S, E is the mirror of V, A is the mirror of Z and D is the mirror of W.
53) SPELL — To get from the code to the word, move the letters in the sequence +3, −5, +3, −5, +3.
54) WASH — This is a mirror code, where the letters are an equal distance from the centre of the alphabet. W is the mirror of D, A is the mirror of Z, S is the mirror of H and H is the mirror of S.
55) HNIY — To get from the word to the code, move the letters in the sequence −5, +5, −5, +5.
56) able — Remove letters 1 and 6, leaving the remaining letters in the order 2, 3, 4, 5.
57) cod — Remove letters 2, 4 and 5, leaving the remaining letters in the order 1, 3, 6.
58) pin — Rearrange letters 1, 2 and 3 in the order 3, 2, 1.
59) sail — Rearrange letters 3, 4, 5 and 6 in the order 6, 3, 4, 5.
60) fade — Remove letters 2 and 3, leaving the remaining letters in the order 1, 4, 5, 6.

Pages 56-60 — Assessment Test 5

1) C — Luke's programme started 30 minutes after Henry's, and Henry's started at 7.30, so Luke's programme cannot have started at 8.10.
2) D — Theo is four years older than Rosie, and Rosie is one year older than Alex, who is 2. Therefore Theo must be five years older than Alex, which makes him 7.
3) 6354 — N = 6, O = 3, D = 5, E = 4
4) 1335 — W = 1, O = 3, O = 3, D = 5
5) NEON — N = 6, E = 4, O = 3, N = 6
6) 6154 — S = 6, L = 1, O = 5, B = 4
7) 6326 — S = 6, A = 3, Y = 2, S = 6
8) BOSS — B = 4, O = 5, S = 6, S = 6
9) fin — Take letters 1, 2 and 3 from the second word.
10) map — Take letters 3 and 2 from the first word, followed by letter 1 from the second word.
11) den — Take letter 1 from the first word, followed by letters 2 and 1 from the second word.
12) dot — Take letters 1 and 2 from the first word, followed by letter 1 from the second word.
13) pine — Take letter 3 from the second word, followed by letters 2 and 3 from the first word, then letter 4 from the second word.
14) EM — The first letter moves forward 3 letters each time. The second letter moves forward 2 letters each time.
15) MX — The first letter moves back 3 letters each time. The second letter moves back 2 letters then 4 letters alternately.
16) IR — The first letter moves forward 3 letters each time. The second letter moves back 3 letters each time.
17) UT — The first letter moves forward 2 letters then 3 letters alternately. The second letter moves forward 1 letter each time.
18) RE — The first letter moves forward one additional letter each time, i.e. +1, +2, +3. The second letter moves forward 2 letters then back 1 letter alternately.
19) f — The new words are 'calf', 'fit', 'loaf' and 'fun'.
20) t — The new words are 'mat', 'trim', 'root' and 'tap'.
21) g — The new words are 'rug', 'gut', 'slug' and 'gas'.

Answers

22) **s** — The new words are 'plus', 'sip', 'bus' and 'sand'.
23) **b** — The new words are 'nib', 'bead', 'sob' and 'ball'.
24) **jewellery   window** — They are examples of things that are made from gold and glass.
25) **sand   ice** — They make up desert and arctic environments.
26) **massive   minute** — They are synonyms of vast and tiny.
27) **success   failure** — They are the outcomes of winning and losing.
28) **sheep   cow** — They are the adult equivalents of lambs and calves.
29) **drop   flake** — They are individual bits of rain and snow.
30) **D** — 4 × 5 − 4 = 16, D = 16
31) **A** — 6 × 4 − 20 = 4, A = 4
32) **A** — 16 ÷ 8 − 1 = 1, A = 1
33) **D** — 25 ÷ 5 + 10 − 2 = 13, D = 13
34) **B** — 21 ÷ 7 × 2 − 2 = 4, B = 4
35) **AGE** — The complete word is CARRIAGE.
36) **OLD** — The complete word is SOLDIER.
37) **ICE** — The complete word is SPICES.
38) **PIN** — The complete word is FLIPPING.
39) **LIE** — The complete word is FAMILIES.
40) **15** — Find the middle point between the two outer numbers by adding the two outer numbers together and dividing the answer by 2.
41) **48** — Multiply the two outer numbers together.
42) **8** — Multiply the first number by 2. Subtract the answer from the third number.
43) **3** — Divide the first number by the third.
44) **7** — Subtract the third number from the first number. Add 1 to the answer.
45) **20** — Add the two outer numbers together. Multiply the answer by 2.
46) **inspire   motivate** — Both words mean 'to fill someone with the urge to do something'.
47) **residue   debris** — Both words mean 'something that remains or is left over'.
48) **plenty   abundance** — Both words mean 'a large quantity'.
49) **answer   reply** — Both words mean 'to respond'.
50) **chase   pursue** — Both words mean 'to follow something in order to catch it'.
51) **overboard** — 'overboard' is the only correctly spelled word that can be made.
52) **beetroot** — 'beetroot' is the only correctly spelled word that can be made.
53) **daylight** — 'daylight' is the only correctly spelled word that can be made.
54) **however** — 'however' is the only correctly spelled word that can be made.
55) **haywire** — 'haywire' is the only correctly spelled word that can be made.
56) **OP** — The first letter in the pair moves back 4 letters, the second letter in the pair moves forward 4 letters.
57) **AZ** — This is a mirror pair, where the letters are an equal distance from the centre of the alphabet. G is 2 letters forward from E, so the answer is AZ because A is 2 letters forward from Y, and Z is its mirror pair.
58) **ML** — The first letter in the pair moves back 1 letter, the second letter in the pair moves back 3 letters.
59) **HW** — The first letter in the pair moves forward 1 letter, the second letter in the pair moves forward 4 letters.
60) **QJ** — This is a mirror pair, where the letters are an equal distance from the centre of the alphabet. S is 3 letters forward from P, so the answer is QJ because Q is 3 letters forward from N, and J is its mirror pair.

Pages 61-65 — Assessment Test 6

1) **Mark** — Mark only has two plans for the future — to live abroad and to go to university.
2) **Jenni** — Jenni likes three flavours of ice cream — vanilla, chocolate and mint.
3) **15** — Subtract 8 each time.
4) **24** — There are two sequences which alternate. In the first sequence, the number doubles each time. In the second, add 5 each time.
5) **48** — Multiply by descending numbers, i.e. ×4, ×3, ×2, ×1.
6) **24** — Add numbers in ascending order: +1, +2, +3, +4, +5.
7) **37** — Add the two previous numbers together, i.e. 4 + 5 = 9, 5 + 9 = 14 etc.
8) **Steph ate** — The hidden word is 'hate'.
9) **year nobody** — The hidden word is 'earn'.
10) **We are** — The hidden word is 'wear'.
11) **Janet chose** — The hidden word is 'etch'.
12) **yoga in** — The hidden word is 'gain'.
13) **k** — The new words are 'sink', 'keen', 'ark' and 'kick'.
14) **d** — The new words are 'led', 'dock', 'thud' and 'dale'.
15) **c** — The new words are 'disc', 'cove', 'talc' and 'cap'.
16) **w** — The new words are 'crow', 'well', 'flaw' and 'wag'.
17) **p** — The new words are 'grip', 'pool', 'lip' and 'pain'.
18) **lose   win** — 'lose' means 'to be unsuccessful', whereas 'win' means 'to be successful'.
19) **above   below** — 'above' means 'at a higher level', whereas 'below' means 'at a lower level'.
20) **borrow   lend** — 'borrow' means 'to take something with the promise of returning it', whereas 'lend' means 'to give something, expecting to get it back'.
21) **selfish   generous** — 'selfish' means 'acting for one's own benefit', whereas 'generous' means 'giving more than is necessary for other people's benefit'.
22) **antique   modern** — 'antique' means 'old', whereas 'modern' means 'new'.
23) **1324** — D = 1, O = 3, V = 2, E = 4
24) **2354** — V = 2, O = 3, L = 5, E = 4
25) **LEAD** — L = 5, E = 4, A = 6, D = 1
26) **1265** — P = 1, O = 2, K = 6, E = 5
27) **3556** — L = 3, E = 5, E = 5, K = 6
28) **LOPE** — L = 3, O = 2, P = 1, E = 5
29) **trip** — 'trip' can mean 'a journey' or 'to catch one's foot on something'.
30) **spell** — 'spell' can mean 'a short amount of time' or 'witchcraft'.
31) **minute** — 'minute' can mean 'very small' or 'a short unit of time'.

32) **fast** — 'fast' can mean 'at high speed' or 'to go without food or drink'.
33) **hollow** — 'hollow' can mean 'without content' or 'a depression in the ground'.
34) **mould** — 'mould' can mean 'to form into a desired shape' or 'a layer of fungi'.
35) **r** — The new words are 'mine' and 'cart'.
36) **c** — The new words are 'rash' and 'crib'.
37) **o** — The new words are 'flat' and 'soon'.
38) **r** — The new words are 'bead' and 'brow'.
39) **p** — The new words are 'pier' and 'pact'.
40) **sad** — Rearrange letters 1, 2 and 4 in the order 4, 2, 1.
41) **pet** — Remove letters 2, 3 and 4, leaving the remaining letters in the order 1, 5, 6.
42) **any** — Remove letters 1 and 4, leaving the remaining letters in the order 2, 3, 5.
43) **lot** — Rearrange letters 2, 3 and 5 in the order 5, 2, 3.
44) **grin** — Rearrange letters 3, 4, 5 and 6 in the order 6, 3, 4, 5.
45) **32** — Multiply the two outer numbers together.
46) **3** — Divide the third number by the first.
47) **17** — Subtract the first number from the third, then add 3.
48) **20** — Add the two outer numbers together, and multiply the answer by 2.
49) **4** — Subtract the third number from the first, then add 1.
50) **29** — 4 × 6 + 5 = 29
51) **24** — 17 − 8 + 15 = 24
52) **9** — 10 × 2 − 4 = 16, 16 = 25 − 9
53) **2** — 18 ÷ 6 × 2 = 6, 6 = 12 ÷ 2
54) **12** — 3 × 3 + 9 = 18, 18 = 12 + 6
55) **17** — 6 × 4 − 9 = 15, 15 = 17 − 2
56) **MVULG** — To get from the word to the code, move the letters in the sequence 0, +1, +2, +3, +4.
57) **CLOCK** — To get from the code to the word, move the letters in the sequence +2, +1, 0, −1, −2.
58) **RLLQO** — To get from the word to the code, move the letters in the sequence −1, −2, −3, −4, −5.
59) **SHEEP** — This is a mirror code, where the letters are an equal distance from the centre of the alphabet. S is the mirror of H, H is the mirror of S, E is the mirror of V and P is the mirror of K.
60) **WHISK** — This is a mirror code, where the letters are an equal distance from the centre of the alphabet. W is the mirror of D, H is the mirror of S, I is the mirror of R, S is the mirror of H and K is the mirror of P.

Pages 66-70 — Assessment Test 7

1) **18** — 24 ÷ 2 − 2 = 10, 10 = 18 − 8
2) **7** — 7 × 4 + 4 = 32, 32 = 25 + 7
3) **2** — 12 × 2 − 16 = 8, 8 = 4 × 2
4) **5** — 2 × 8 ÷ 4 = 4, 4 = 9 − 5
5) **6** — 20 ÷ 4 × 3 = 15, 15 = 9 + 6
6) **alone   together** — 'alone' means 'by yourself', whereas 'together' means 'with other people'.
7) **early   delayed** — 'early' means 'before the expected time', whereas 'delayed' means 'later than expected'.
8) **smile   frown** — A 'smile' is a facial expression showing pleasure, whereas a 'frown' is a facial expression showing displeasure.
9) **windy   still** — 'windy' means 'lots of wind', whereas 'still' means 'no wind'.
10) **awake   asleep** — 'awake' means 'conscious', whereas 'asleep' means 'unconscious'.
11) **C** — 5 × 3 − 13 + 3 = 5, C = 5
12) **D** — 25 × 2 − 25 − 4 = 21, D = 21
13) **E** — 21 − 10 + 3 + 7 = 21, E = 21
14) **D** — 18 ÷ 6 × 4 + 4 = 16, D = 16
15) **B** — 24 ÷ 8 × 4 − 8 = 4, B = 4
16) **OUR** — The complete word is POURED.
17) **VAN** — The complete word is ADVANCED.
18) **ACT** — The complete word is FACTORY.
19) **NAP** — The complete word is SNAPPED.
20) **PIN** — The complete word is SPINNING.
21) **RAM** — The complete word is GRAMMAR.
22) **river   stream** — The other three are all still bodies of water.
23) **television   stereo** — The other three are all used with a computer.
24) **shawl   fan** — The other three are all items for keeping dry in the rain.
25) **hymn   lullaby** — The other three are all types of poem.
26) **India   China** — The other three are all countries in Europe.
27) **QY** — The first letter moves forward 5 letters each time. The second letter moves forward 3 letters each time.
28) **KC** — The first letter moves in the sequence −1, 0, +1, +2, +3. The second letter moves back 2 letters then forward 1 letter alternately.
29) **VF** — The first letter moves back 5 letters each time. The second letter moves forward 4 letters then back 2 letters alternately.
30) **TS** — The first letter moves forward one additional letter each time, i.e. +1, +2, +3, +4. The second letter moves forward one additional letter each time, i.e. 0, +1, +2, +3.
31) **JR** — The first letter moves forward 1 letter, then forward 2 letters alternately. The second letter moves back 1 letter, then back 2 letters alternately.
32) **t** — The new words are 'rust' and 'tore'.
33) **r** — The new words are 'bush' and 'fern'.
34) **h** — The new words are 'clot' and 'shell'.
35) **r** — The new words are 'daft' and 'drew'.
36) **m** — The new words are 'stop' and 'comb'.
37) **shock   calmness** — They are synonyms of 'alarm' and 'peace'.
38) **liberty   confinement** — They are synonyms of 'freedom' and 'captivity'.
39) **honesty   deception** — They are the moral attributes of telling the truth and lying.
40) **stop   go** — They are synonyms of 'stall' and 'advance'.
41) **tomorrow   today** — They are the days that follow today and yesterday.
42) **6431** — T = 6, O = 4, I = 3, L = 1
43) **1446** — L = 1, O = 4, O = 4, T = 6

44) **LIFT** — L = 1, I = 3, F = 5, T = 6
45) **5516** — E = 5, E = 5, L = 1, S = 6
46) **1543** — L = 1, E = 5, A = 4, D = 3
47) **SEAL** — S = 6, E = 5, A = 4, L = 1
48) **D** — Sam is silent for 5 minutes longer than Alice, who is silent for 4 minutes less than Ellie. Therefore Sam is silent for 1 minute longer than Ellie.
49) **E** — Four of the five towns have a theatre, but Corford doesn't, which means that Batston must. Since Elming is the only town that has both a sports centre and a theatre, Batston cannot have a sports centre.
50) **rat** — Rearrange letters 2, 3 and 4 in the order 4, 2, 3.
51) **and** — Remove letters 1, 2 and 5, leaving the remaining letters in the order 3, 4, 6.
52) **raw** — Rearrange letters 2, 3 and 4 in the order 3, 2, 4.
53) **neat** — Rearrange letters 2, 3, 5 and 6 in the order 5, 2, 6, 3.
54) **lead** — Rearrange letters 1, 2, 5 and 6 in the order 5, 6, 2, 1.
55) **YS** — The first letter in the pair moves back 3 letters, the second letter moves forward 5 letters.
56) **BQ** — The first letter in the pair moves forward 4 letters, the second letter moves back 3 letters.
57) **XL** — The first letter in the pair moves back 4 letters, the second letter moves forward 2 letters.
58) **FU** — This is a mirror code, where the letters are an equal distance from the centre of the alphabet. V is 2 letters back from X, so the answer is FU because F is 2 letters back from H, and U is its mirror pair.
59) **WA** — The first letter in the pair moves back 4 letters, the second letter moves forward 2 letters.
60) **PK** — This is a mirror code, where the letters are an equal distance from the centre of the alphabet. N is 3 letters forward from K, so the answer is PK because P is 3 letters forward from M, and K is its mirror pair.

Answers

Progress Chart

Use this chart to keep track of your scores for the <u>Assessment Tests</u>.

You can do each test more than once — download extra answer sheets from cgpbooks.co.uk/11plus/answer-sheets or scan the QR code on the right.

Answer Sheets

	First Go	Second Go	Third Go
Test 1	Date: Score:	Date: Score:	Date: Score:
Test 2	Date: Score:	Date: Score:	Date: Score:
Test 3	Date: Score:	Date: Score:	Date: Score:
Test 4	Date: Score:	Date: Score:	Date: Score:
Test 5	Date: Score:	Date: Score:	Date: Score:
Test 6	Date: Score:	Date: Score:	Date: Score:
Test 7	Date: Score:	Date: Score:	Date: Score:

Look back at your scores once you've done all the <u>Assessment Tests</u>.
Each test is out of <u>60 marks</u>.

Work out which kind of mark you scored most often:

0-35 marks — Go back to <u>basics</u> and work on your <u>question technique</u>.

36-50 marks — You're nearly there — go back over the questions you found <u>tricky</u>.

51-60 marks — You're a <u>Verbal Reasoning star</u>. Go on to <u>Practice Book Age 10-11</u>.